D1233326

Flying High

Flying High

SPUD WEBB
with Reid Slaughter

1817

HARPER & ROW, PUBLISHERS, New York
Cambridge, Philadelphia, San Francisco
London, Mexico City, São Paulo, Singapore, Sydney

To Katie and David, Joanie and Lee
with love
Whatever we have accomplished,
it is because of you

FIRST EDITION

Designer: Erich Hobbing
Copy editor: Gretchen Gordon

Library of Congress Cataloging-in-Publication Data

Webb, Spud.
  Flying high.

  1. Webb, Spud.   2. Basketball players—United
States—Biography.   I. Slaughter, Reid.   II. Title.
GV884.W35A3   1988   796.32'3'0924 [B]   87-45084
ISBN 0-06-015820-4

---

88 89 90 91 92 DT/ RRD 10 9 8 7 6 5 4 3 2 1

Contents

Foreword
by Julius Erving

The first time I met Anthony "Spud" Webb was in 1981 during a trip to Dallas to play the expansion team Mavericks at Reunion Arena. My coach, Billy Cunningham, had heard about him at Midland Junior College and called Spud's mother's home to leave him a couple of tickets for the game. Apparently Spud's older brother did not believe it was Billy on the phone and began quizzing him about what our record had been the year before. Spud came to the game and worked his way back to the locker room and stood with some of the other kids who were waiting for autographs. I can remember extending my arm to shake the hand of this shy, soft-spoken kid and exchanging the usual "nice to meet you." It was five years later, when the 76ers were playing a preseason exhibition game against the Atlanta Hawks in Birmingham, Alabama, that I next saw Spud. Walking along the bench to greet the veterans and meet the rookies I said hello to Dominique Wilkins and Randy Wittman. On the end of the bench, sitting between 7'1" Tree Rollins and 7'0" Jon Koncak, was that same shy, soft-spoken kid, Spud. I again extended my hand and said, "Congratulations, Spud, welcome to the league." Four months later Spud, at 5'7", would rock the world and win the 1986 N.B.A. Slam Dunk Championship, a title that I had won in the first-ever contest more than 15 years before.

In the early days of my own career many people labeled me as a slam dunk specialist. I did not invent the dunk, but writers have credited me with making it famous. Spud has added another dimension to the dunk—but it is not Spud's dunking ability that makes him special. It has always been very important to me to work on all dimensions of my game and to strive to be a complete person off the court as well. I am proud of Spud's involvement in community services and with kids. In only two years in the league Spud has actively involved himself with numerous charities, including the Boys Club, the Cystic Fibrosis Foundation, the Lupus Foundation, and children's hospitals across the country. He has also donated his time for antidrug campaigns and has spoken at many free clinics for kids. Spud loves kids, and my own little girl, Jazmin, is one of his biggest fans.

I am honored that Spud has looked up to me as an athlete and a role model. His abilities are God-given, and he should never abuse them. However, I am more honored by the fact that Spud is giving something back to the kids and is working just as hard on being a complete person as he is on being a complete player. That desire gives great depth and meaning to the real ability to fly high. I wish for Spud a tremendous career and pray that he continues to trust in the Lord and to give back a portion of that which has been given to him. Just as the game of basketball is more than a dunk . . . so is the game of life so much more than basketball.

Preface

Spud Webb is a tough guy to figure. Despite all evidence to the contrary, he somehow developed the notion that he could one day play pro basketball. Never mind that everyone laughed at the idea, at the sheer absurdity of a 5'6" (or so) waterbug challenging the giants of the NBA. Spud Webb went out and did exactly that.

It wasn't the first remarkable thing that Spud had done. In fact, his life before the professional sports fishbowl had a trophy case full of other dramatic moments, the kind great movies (and yes, books) are made from. And so, when I first approached Spud about doing a book on his life, it seemed a foregone conclusion that he would say yes.

He said no.

Where most pro athletes—or anyone else, for that matter—would be flattered to have their stories written, Spud shrugged off the idea. He suggested we go play one-on-one instead.

Using my four-inch height advantage and my fourteen-inch vertical leap (Spud's, by the way, is forty-two inches), I managed to score exactly three points in a game to fifteen. The humiliation probably would have continued, except that a group of kids recognized Spud and seized the opportunity to mob him for autographs.

I watched as Spud talked to those kids, answering their questions and throwing out a joke or two. Most of all, he was patient with them, the way so few adults are these days, listening to them and delighting in their company. It was the perfect moment.

"Spud, this is why you have to do the book," I said, looking at the growing sea of people moving toward him. "These people want to know how somebody their size achieved the dream." He smiled, and the book was under way.

The year I spent with Spud was revealing and inspiring, but two stories stand out in my mind as guideposts to Spud's character and unique sense of humility as a pro athlete. Believe it or not, several people told me not to put these in the book. "Those stories are too 'goodie-goodie' for people to handle. It'll be a turnoff," they advised. Well, I'll take my chances. I think the sports public could use a couple of heartening anecdotes.

The first comes from Jim Valvano, the fiery NC State basketball czar who coached Spud through his junior and senior seasons.

"Every year, some of our former basketball team stars drop in on us and we roll out the red carpet," says Valvano. "We get them hotel rooms, tickets to a NC State home football game, take 'em out to eat—everything. We also introduce them to the high school recruits, which helps our recruiting.

"So I'm at our home game against East Carolina in the fall of 1985, and I'm introducing a handful of recruits to some of our former players, giving them the full 'conquering hero comes home' buildup. All of a sudden I see this little guy standing behind them, and it's Spud! I said, 'Spud, what in the world are you doing here? Why didn't you call?'

" 'Aw, Coach,' he said, 'I just dropped in.'

" 'But how did you get a ticket?' I asked.

" 'Bought one,' said Spud.

" 'Well, Spud, do you need a place to stay or a car to use?'

" 'Hey, Coach V, don't worry about me,' he laughed. 'It's no big deal.'

"I knew I had to do something, because Spud was so popular at NC State he deserved a proper homecoming. So I went up to the press box, got on the public address system, and announced to the entire crowd, 'Ladies and gentlemen, we have a very special guest here today. Visiting us is one of the greatest players in NC State basketball history, now a star with the Atlanta Hawks of the NBA . . . Mr. Spud Webb!'

"With that, all 56,000 people stood and cheered like crazy, interrupting the game for three full minutes while they gave Spud a standing ovation."

The other story took place almost a year later, during the off-season. Spud was in Portland, competing in a slam dunk contest held by the Trailblazers. He had agreed to do a personal appearance afterward at G.I. Joe's, a local department store. The appearance was supposed to be the standard two hours of signing autographs, shaking hands, and posing for pictures. It turned out to be something very special.

When Spud arrived at the store, more than 300 people were already in line awaiting the basketball star's appearance. He made his way into the store, where the line of fans continued to the back of the store. After two hours, the line had not shortened—in fact, it had gotten *longer*. The store manager walked over to Spud and said, "Listen, we never expected this many people. That line is more than an hour long, so I understand if you want to leave."

"Are you kidding?" said Spud, and he continued to sign autographs for every person. Then, toward the end, a small boy walked up and asked Spud to sign his shoes. Spud noticed the boy was wearing Adidas, and he told the boy, "Listen, I'm sorry, but I endorse Pony shoes, and I wouldn't feel right about signing another brand." With sad eyes the boy looked up at his mother. He was far too young to understand about marketing contracts and product loyalty. "You mean, I can't have your autograph?" he asked.

Spud paused for a moment, and then he took the Pony sneakers off his own feet, signed them, and gave them to the little boy. The little boy was overcome, shrieking with joy and hugging the shoes to his chest like a newfound treasure. And when Spud finally left the store *four* hours later, he walked out in his socks.

This book is much more than a basketball story. It's a book about believing in yourself. It's about faith and hard work and family—the cornerstones of what we sometimes call the American Dream. Spud Webb tells us that we can do anything we want to do if we're willing to work for it. His story has touched my life, and I hope through these pages it will touch millions more. Spud may be little on the outside, but inside he is larger than life.

Acknowledgments

A successful book, like a good lasagna recipe, has a lot go into it. This effort is no different, and Spud and I are most appreciative to several people who proved to be key ingredients.

First and foremost, thanks to our editor, Daniel Bial of Harper & Row, for his endless good faith. Though as hopelessly mediocre at basketball as myself, Bial made the book soar with his keen insight and good humor. For this he deserves a window in his office, even a small one. Additional editing was very capably handled by Gretchen Gordon.

Even before the publisher, there is the agent, and Jan Miller provided unending enthusiasm and worked hard every step of the way. For a new author, there is nothing more valuable. More thanks to Jan's colleague Sandra Bredeson, who tirelessly worked through the early drafts.

I could never have done this book without a long year of patience and understanding from the staff at *Park Cities People*. They proved to me why they are the best weekly newspaper staff in the country, and my partner and confidant, Jim Wilson, gave leadership that I could never repay him for. Four others at the paper who deserve particular mention are Betsy Reppeto, Phil Stephens, Glenda Vosburgh, and the old sailor himself, Tom McCartin.

Debby Slaughter, the kind of sister every boy dreams about, was helpful in a number of ways, and she has my thanks and my love.

The whole gang at Talent Sports International were wonderful, and Spud and I both can't say enough about Lauri Harjo, Clark Wolfsberger, Carmen Stocker, and David Smigel. Craig Massey, who first pitched the book idea, was continually inspirational, as only he can be.

Big hugs for all the members of the Webb family: Katie, David, Janice, Bean, Renee, Stephanie (the family photographer), and Reg. And then there's Bobby, B. J., and Amber as well. Lots of people in the neighborhood gave interviews and were helpful, including Charles Lewis, Derrick Leonard, Dawn Baker, Ertis Rogers, and Alvin Jordan.

A special thanks to Ken Sins, who saved the day with additional material on Spud's NC State career.

More friends who deserve thanks are Terry Wilson and her smiling threesome of Loren, Katie, and Jamie; Rick Lafitte and the gang at Cornerstone; Brad Martin, Peter Bell, Katie Ryan Blakeley, Jeff Blakeley, Pete Adams, and Carolyn Ryburn.

Many friends in the media helped out with articles, photographs, and information. I'm grateful to Louis DeLuca, Skip Hollandsworth, Carlton Stowers, and Eddie Perkins. Tremendous assistance was given by Jeff Denberg and Rich Addicks of the *Atlanta Journal/Constitution*.

The entire Atlanta Hawks organization was wonderful, and I know Spud means it when he says he doesn't want to play anywhere else. Big thanks to p.r. whiz Bill Needle and his staff, to Stan Kasten, coach Mike Fratello, and his assistants, Willis Reed and Brendan Suhr. And thanks to all the Hawk players who sat very patiently and talked about their teammate. Several other NBA players gave interviews, and so my thanks to Magic Johnson, Joe Dumars, Karl Malone, Rolando Blackman, and Dennis Rodman. Of course, special mention to that special man, Julius Erving.

Finally, the biggest thanks goes to Robin Blakeley, Spud's agent, who is a shining example of what everyone in that profession should be. The most loyal friend, infinitely creative, hard-working to a fault, and not a bad outside jump shot—Robin has it all, and this book is as much for him as anyone.

1

Taking Off

I'm black, I'm twenty-four years old, and most of the time I think I'm the luckiest guy on earth. I play the game I love —basketball—with the world's greatest players and I get paid for it. Remarkable.

It is remarkable because playing in the NBA was always my dream, a pretty ambitious dream for a guy my size. Standing in the shower I'm 5'6" tall, but when I'm on the basketball court I'm much taller—5'7" to be exact, thanks to my Pony shoes and a thick pair of socks. Sportswriters like to point out that I'm more than a foot shorter than the NBA average (6'7½"), but the truth is I never let that bother me. I don't look up, I look ahead.

Every day there's a new challenge. Sometimes it's a big game, sometimes it's just trying to live a good life. But on February 8, 1986, my challenge was to win the NBA Slam Dunk Championship. Like most of the things in my life, I had to go about it the hard way.

For some reason, my name wasn't at the top of the list when the league office considered which eight players would be selected to compete in the contest. In fact, at first

I wasn't even on the list, but Michael Jordan was injured and thanks to about a hundred letters from my agent, the league decided to give a little guy a try.

Time out for a minute. I want to talk about being small.

Everybody talks about my size, and I realize that being short is the obvious thing that sets me apart from other pro basketball players. People see me standing next to one of my teammates, like Tree Rollins (7'1") or Kevin Willis (7'), and they can't believe it. Let's face it, it looks funny. But to me, size is just that—an appearance. You know, sometimes you'll be out and see old folks dancing up a storm and think, "Wow, they're sure dancing fast for old folks." Or maybe you see some blind person like Ray Charles or Stevie Wonder cranking out a mean tune on the piano and think, "Gosh, it's amazing he can do that." Well, I look at my size the same way—I don't think about being small, I just think about what I want to do and go do it.

If you want to do something, I mean really want to do it, you've just got to set your mind that you can achieve that goal. I don't care what it is. It's not true when you're driving a car or skiing down a hill, but for most things in life, it's more important to see the possibilities, not the obstacles. People spend way too much time worrying about *why* they can't do something instead of just going out and *doing* it.

One other point. I love basketball so much you can't believe it. It's the greatest game in the world and (now I hope Hawks president Stan Kasten doesn't bring this up the next time we negotiate a contract) I'd play for free. I'm gonna play as long as I can and, who knows, maybe they'll even have basketball in heaven!

There's a passage in a book I was reading called *The Lords of Discipline* that expresses really well how I feel about basketball. The book is about a black guy who goes to a Southern military school. The rest of the cadets are white, and they all give him a hard time except this one basketball player. Basketball is his "high," his escape from all the political stuff going on at school. Getting ready for his very last game the player looks around the empty gym and thinks:

> Has there ever been a boy who loved this game as much as I have loved it? I had known the praise of the crowds and knew nothing else on earth to equal it. When I played basketball, I was possessed by a nakedness of spirit, an absolute purity, a divine madness when I was let loose to ramble between the lines. Always, I was reckless and moving at full speed . . . I had learned that my grace came only in the full abandoned divinity of flight.

For me, pursuing a basketball career with all my heart and soul was just that easy—the game is that much fun.

And I'm not the only one who has that feeling. That's why so many of us in the NBA keep playing even after the season is over—because we love to get out there and do our thing, mixing it up, dancing and dunking up and down the floor.

As a kid my idol was Julius Erving, so I guess it's no shock that I worked hard trying to learn how to dunk a basektball. Watching him on TV, taking off from the free-throw line and floating, higher and higher, until he was almost looking down into the basket, then slamming the ball through the hoop with such force . . . all I knew is that I wanted to know that feeling. I wanted to fly like Dr. J, be graceful like him.

And like him, I've always wanted to be thought of as a great basketball player *first*, and a dunker second. For me, the two talents are very separate. Basketball is a game with many different elements requiring lots of mental toughness and concentration, while dunking is just showmanship with a little athletic talent thrown in. That doesn't mean it's easy, because making great dunks is something you have to practice a lot. I know; I practiced my dunks *thousands* of times for years before I ever walked onto the court on that All-Star Saturday. I always put basketball before dunking, but after we finished playing in high school and in college I would hang around the gym and start jammin'.

For all you folks with White Man's Disease (that's just the playful way we brothers refer to an inability to jump), I'll tell you that dunking *is* enjoyable—as much fun to do as it is to watch. If you've never done it, let me assure you that soaring up to the basket feels as close to flying as you can get, without jumping off a roof or falling out of a plane. So that's what my objective was in Dallas: have some fun, win the contest, and definitely surprise a few people.

The Slam Dunk contest not only surprised the public, it surprised my teammates. Sure, I had done a few basic dunks during the season, but never anything fancy at all. In fact, I don't think any of the Hawks had ever seen me do any show dunks, and when word came out that I was in the contest, they kidded me about what I might do so I wouldn't embarrass myself in front of the Reunion Arena crowd.

The worst razzing took place in the Cleveland airport one morning after we had just beaten the Cavaliers in a thriller, 105–104. Randy Wittman had tipped in a missed bucket with only a second to go and it was a great win, so everybody was feeling good.

"Hey Dominique, what's it gonna take to win the Slam Dunk this year, man?" asked Cliff Levingston.

4

My teammate, the man sometimes known as "The Human Highlight Film" because of his awesome talents, felt sure he'd win the contest easily.

"Same thing it took last year," said 'Nique with a smile. "Say, Spud, what are you gonna do?"

"Don't you guys worry about me," I replied.

"But we *are* worried, Spud," 'Nique said. "I think what you ought to do is get a ladder. We'll set it up in the paint. It don't have to be a big ladder. What you do is, run up the ladder, jump off, and do a three-sixty [a full spin]—people will go crazy, man! You know how it is, they'll laugh and say that ladder is twenty feet tall!"

"No, wait, I got it!" shouted Tree. (That's Tree Rollins, who got his nickname because that's what he's as big as.) "Wear a cape! Get a cape with a big S on it—the judges will love it. Hell, Spud, I'll buy it for you!"

I remember thinking to myself, "These guys are making a big joke out of this, but it isn't a joke. I can do things they don't know about. None of these guys know what I can do."

My chance to prove that came soon enough.

The day before the contest I wasn't actually nervous, probably because I didn't have time to be. I was scheduled to appear on the *Tonight Show* with Johnny Carson, which meant I had to catch a flight to Los Angeles, do the show, then hightail it back to Dallas that same night. I got to L.A. about half an hour before taping for the show started, so they flew me in a helicopter to the Carson studios in Burbank. Now *that* was scary. In an airplane, if you look straight ahead, you see a plane full of people reading magazines; but in a helicopter, all you see is *the ground*. After that experience, doing the show was easy.

And it was fun. Johnny showed some NBA clips of me playing and started asking questions. It's funny, but you don't really think about all the millions of television viewers because Johnny makes you feel that it's just the two of you sitting around, having a conversation. During the break he asked me about all the traveling NBA players do, and I told him it was tiring but still fun for me since I was new in the league. After the break, he started joking around and asked me about meeting women on the road. That cracked me up. I started laughing, and then he said, "Tell me when you're blushing, will you?" Another big roar. Carson is a great guy and I can see why he's been so successful for so long. He makes it easy to be your best.

Flying back to Dallas, it started to sink in: I had just been on the Johnny Carson show! Here's something I'd watched a thousand times in my living room at home, and suddenly it's *me* there being interviewed! I just couldn't believe it. I had to admit, this fame stuff was a little embarrassing sometimes, but it sure was fun.

The morning of the Slam Dunk Contest I told myself I was going to win. Then I packed my gear and went to breakfast. I ate with my coach from Midland Junior College, Jerry Stone, and John Cinecola, the marketing director for Pony Shoes (which I endorse). They gave me lots of encouragement, and I headed over to Reunion Arena to watch the first event of the day, the Legends Classic. From the moment those stars walked on the court, the fans were appreciative, and there was much to appreciate. The game tipped off and the hands of time went back twenty years as names like Cousy, Robertson, Havlicek, and Maravich moved casually (if not totally gracefully) up and down the court. I stood by as Walt Frazier went up for a jump shot and I felt invigorated by his presence. These were the greats, the men who gave modern basketball its tradition. To see them play was as reassuring as it was entertaining.

Memories tumbled over one another as the announcer called the game, and two names in particular caught my attention: Slater Martin and Calvin Murphy. Although

Martin is white and now 60 years old, while Murphy is black and only 37, the two men share some common denominators that I relate to: Both are small men who played a big man's game (Martin is 5'10", Murphy 5'9"), and both men are Texans. Martin had been a standout at the University of Texas during the postwar years and had played on five NBA world championship teams, four in Minneapolis and one in St. Louis. Martin came back to the Lone Star state in the early '60s and coached the Houston ABA franchise before getting into the restaurant business in Houston, where he lives today.

While Slater was considered on the small side during his playing days, Calvin Murphy was "the Spud Webb of the '70s," the guy everyone said could never play pro ball. He had piled up some incredible stats at Niagara University, but it wasn't until he made the NBA All-Rookie team as a member of the Houston Rockets in 1971 that people began giving him credit. He went on to play 13 seasons averaging almost 18 points per game, and even made the All-Star team. Calvin is a great guy and he works with kids down in Houston. I spoke to him and Slater before the Slam Dunk contest, and they both said it was nice to see there was still room for a little guy in the NBA. They wished me luck in the contest, saying "Go ahead, Spud, take it to those big boys."

Next was the Long Distance Shoot-Out. The winner— to no one's surprise—was Larry Bird. What was amazing was the *way* he won it, sinking 18 for 25, rapid-fire (including 11 shots in a row at one point), from 3-point range! I'll tell you, even though you play against these pro players 100 nights a year, you're still amazed at the skills some of these guys have and you wonder how they do what they do.

Now it was time to show what *I* could do. Stretching out before the first dunk, I spotted Bill Needle, director of public relations for the Hawks. He had made the trip to provide some moral support, which meant a lot. He called me over and made a suggestion.

"Spud, before you make your first dunk, why not go stand under the basket, so everyone can get an idea of just how high you've got to jump to get up there?"

It was a great idea, and I did just that. Looking up at the basket, I was like a mountain climber surveying the summit; I had done this thousands of times before, but never before 17,000 people and a few million more on TV. I was really nervous.

The butterflies left just as my double-pump reverse slam went through the hoop. It's an old favorite, and it felt good. The judges gave me a 46 out of a possible 50, the best score of the first set of dunks. Still, the crowd wasn't hollering much and that almost made me laugh because I realized, "These people don't expect me to do this." Well, as you'll see throughout this book, the best way to get me to do something is to make it clear you think I *can't* do it —I love that challenge. In the next two dunks, I did a one-handed 360 and a double-pump straight ahead jam that gave me a total of 141 points, the best of round 1. In round 2, my competition would be my teammate Dominique Wilkins and his brother Gerald (who plays for the New York Knicks) and Terrance Stansbury of the Indiana Pacers.

Leading off in round 2, I decided to do something spectacular. It was a timing dunk, where I throw the ball ahead of me in a high arc, then catch the ball near the basket at the peak of its bounce, then whirl around and reverse slam it behind my head. The throw, the bounce, the slam—they went perfectly and the crowd went wild. The judges gave the dunk a 50 and I felt fantastic! As a teenager I practiced these dunks over and over in rec centers and old falling-down high school gyms, saying to myself, "Now here's

Spud Webb, the famous NBA star, going up for a big dunk in the Slam Dunk Contest . . . he bounces the ball, he grabs it in midair . . . and he jams it! The crowd goes wild over Webb! What a dunk!" Man, I had that dream so many times, and now here I was, living it! Still, the funniest thing about this was the look on my teammates' faces —those guys who had come "to make sure I didn't embarrass myself," Cliff Levingston and Tree Rollins, were in shock. I think Dominique was surprised too, but it didn't stop him from giving the crowd a few more thrills. He followed me with a "nuclear roundhouse tomahawk" dunk that brought down the house.

Two dunks later, Dominique and I were in the finals and Reunion Arena was rocking. The noise on the floor was deafening and adrenaline was pumping through my body like a steam engine. I felt the crowd, filled with my friends and family, pull together around me as I stood at midcourt, preparing for the first dunk of the finals. My mind was racing: Which one should I do? Crazy thing is, it was hard to decide 'cause I was having so much fun.

My life did a complete turnaround that afternoon, so it was appropriate that I chose a 360, starting out from the right side and ending on the left with a one-handed jam, which is hard for me because I can't palm the ball. Yep, I've got short fingers, too. That didn't matter when the ball went through the net. As I "came down to earth" the thunder was beginning, with fans stomping their feet and waving cards with "10" printed on them so furiously you could almost feel a breeze. Nothing beats having the hometown folks behind you, and they wanted a perfect score; good for me they got it.

Great players always rise to the occasion, and my buddy 'Nique is definitely a great player, not to mention the reigning Slam Dunk champ. He showed his stuff on the next dunk, a soaring windmill 360 that no one does as well as 'Nique. The fans and the judges knew it was special, and I was glad they gave it the perfect 50 it deserved. Now there was one dunk left.

There's nothing quite like a crowd hushed in anticipation. You've got them in your hand, and you know if you do something spectacular, they're going to go crazy. I guess that's why I chose a timing dunk—an over-the-rim, off-the-backboard, one-handed slam, which arched just right. I was so charged up that I got higher than expected and almost crash-landed on the Reunion floor. But when I hit the boards and heard the reaction, I somehow knew I would win. It was pandemonium, and I couldn't stop a huge smile from taking over my face. Dominique followed with a perfect double-pump, two-handed jackknife and I thought we might tie, which would have been great. Still, they gave him a 48 and yours truly was the 1986 Slam Dunk Champion. They announced my name, and I ran over to hug Dominique. I was glad to have my best friend there to share my happiness, even if he had to lose. It was an incredible moment, and after they presented me with the trophy and the $12,000 check, I was hoisted up onto the rim of the basket. I looked out over the crowd and thought how lucky I was, and how grateful I felt to God for this moment. Thanks to Him, the little guy had beaten the odds yet again.

2

The Beetleweight Champion
of the World

Why would anybody name their kid "Spud"? Well, the truth be known, my parents named me Anthony, and my famous nickname was the creation of Mr. Rufus "Buster" Daniels, a close family friend. And despite what you might think, the name has nothing to do with potatoes but rather with the shape of my head when I was a baby.

The story goes that the day after I was born, some friends and relatives were at the house checking me out when Buster suggested that my head looked like Sputnik, the Russian satellite. (Now, later in life, it's been suggested I've "launched into space" a few times off the basketball court, but I've never picked up any Russian television broadcasts.) My sister didn't know anything about satellites, but they thought the name sounded cool, and in the funny way that kids talk it became "Spud." My older brother, David Webb, Jr., had the same treatment, and today everyone calls him "Bean." I guess we've got some weirdly shaped heads in the Webb family. Anyway, at least people don't call me by my middle name—Jerome.

West Dallas is a ravaged, dangerous place today, but it was somewhat better in the 1950s when my parents moved there from Louisiana. Wood-frame houses crowded the streets, and here and there you would find a poorly managed apartment building with kids running in and out while old men and young men alike watched lazily from their front-porch vantage points. Most of the city's middle-class black families lived there, and even though we referred to it as The Projects it wasn't a ghetto. The decline came right as my family outgrew our little place, which had three tiny bedrooms and two bathrooms. We lived in West Dallas—all eight of us—until I was five years old. Yes, it was crowded, but being in a big family was fun, and the close quarters brought us together as kids.

I've got five brothers and sisters all together. My oldest sister, Janice, ran the show. Strong and dependable, she was a model first child, almost like a second mother. Renee came next, two years younger than Janice. Bright and outgoing, Renee tried out for everything—and usually made it. A year later came Stephanie, the third straight girl. Stephanie is someone who speaks her mind, and she has always been a great athlete.

After Steph my mom had three boys. Bean, or David Jr., is the nicest guy in the world, quiet and passive, kind of a pushover but a good role model for me. I came four years after Bean and was followed by Reg, the baby, who came three years after me. Reg was spoiled pretty well, like most babies, but he grew up to be a great athlete and is now in college on a track scholarship.

My parents were strong, positive role models for us kids. My father, David Webb, Sr., had started working when he was only nine. Every day after school, he went over to the grocery store and worked until way past closing time. His friends would kid him about working so hard, but by the time he was fourteen he had saved enough money to buy his parents a house, which he still owns today. The son of a minister, Dad has never had a drink in his life, and as we grew up he was always telling us that we should never get in with people who were drinking or using drugs—he hated that stuff. He was also a pretty good athlete, and he still holds several track records at his alma mater, Doyline High School, in Doyline, Louisiana. After high school, he played baseball for the Minden Giants of the old Negro League but later gave that up to move to a town he saw as the place of opportunity—Dallas.

Before he moved, he met a pretty lady named Katie Platt, who was valedictorian of her junior high class and a high school honor graduate. They got married and headed to the Big D, where Dad worked two jobs. In the morning he was at Brencato's Grocery in North Dallas, and by night he was the butcher and cashier at a Speedy Mart close to Fair Park and the Cotton Bowl.

With six kids running all over the place, my parents were concerned about the neighborhood we were growing up in. They decided the family would move away from the escalating crime rate of the inner city to South Dallas, a rural area far from the fast city pace. We knew it was a good move for us, but I cried saying good-bye to my kindergarten friends, and my brothers and sisters had tearful good-byes as well. After all, we were not only leaving our friends behind but also moving to a new school district where we didn't know anybody.

South Dallas looked deserted. Our house was only the second to be built as part of a new housing development, and there were big fields in every direction. It was like going from *Good Times* to *Hee-Haw*. My brothers and sisters and I didn't realize it then, but in those little houses along all those dusty back roads were many other great families like ours, with more talent and community spirit than any place we'd ever been. It was a place where we could flourish and excel.

In a family of achievers, Dad led the way. The white man who owned the Speedy Mart recognized Dad's ambition and approached him one day with an offer.

"David, business isn't too good, as you know. This neighborhood is changing, and I think you could do a better job than I can with this store. Do you want to take over?"

Dad said yes, and they arranged for him to buy the store.

I was now 12 years old, and I remember what a big day it was for all of us when our family officially took over ownership of the store. Dad renamed it "Webb's Soul Mart" and made several changes that fit the name. He added soul food to the menu—things like chitlins, neck bones, and boudin (spicy sausage with rice). He started selling records, clothes, and gifts as well as groceries. And he put a couple of pool tables against one wall of the store, where I sharpened my pool game. The place soon became a neighborhood hangout.

There weren't a lot of white people in West Dallas or South Dallas. For a long time not only were all my friends black, but I didn't even meet that many white people. That's changed since, of course, but as a kid I wasn't really affected by the frequent incidents of racism I've heard some friends and teammates talk about. My South Dallas neighborhood was made up mostly of hard-working, decent families, and I've always been proud to be black.

I certainly wouldn't say we were rich when I was growing up, but I wouldn't say we were poor, either. My father's business went well. There was food on the table and cars in the driveway, and some extra money was always around if I needed a new baseball glove or if an emergency arose. My whole family went to church regularly. Although I can recall sometimes staring at the ceiling, anxiously waiting for the service to end so I could go out and play ball, I also grew to love my religion and to believe deeply. The sound of the choir singing, Reverend Jenkins's raspy voice preaching away, and people crying "Amen!" —all this helped bring me closer to God. My parents believed that you had to love your God and work hard in order to live the right kind of life. I haven't always agreed with everything they've said, but what I've seen in life tells me they were absolutely right on that score.

It was pretty obvious from the beginning that I was never going to play middle linebacker for the Dallas Cowboys. I was scrawny—always the smallest kid in any group. I also had a scrawny friend, Charles Lewis, but mostly I hung around with guys much bigger than I was. Being the smallest was something I slowly began to accept, yet it frustrated me. I always thought that if I were just *a little bit* bigger, I could be a much better athlete. This frustration made me a hardheaded, sometimes moody kid. If people made fun of my size, I got angry. If they said I would fail because of my size, I became stubborn, and determined to prove them wrong. I would throw myself into every sport I played, giving everything I could to prove my value, and still I felt that the bigger, stronger athletes got all the breaks. Why was I so small? I knew that if I could just get bigger, then all my problems would be solved.

Alvin Jordan showed me how wrong I was. Alvin ran the Turnkey Boys Club, which was just a couple of blocks from my house and which soon became my second home. A looming, serious man, Alvin laid down the law with us kids and didn't tolerate any monkey business, but he also had a knack for making things fun, and lots of youngsters in the neighborhood gave up "hanging out with the tough guys" to come join the Boys Club. Since I was only 10 at the time, and my dad was gone most of the time working, much of what I learned about life and how to be a responsible kid came from Alvin. We played every kind of sport you can imagine, from Ping-Pong and Foosball to football and basketball. From time to time, Alvin would bring in former sports stars to talk to us about staying away from alcohol and drugs. That worked, too. Some big basketball hero would come by, and the next week you'd see guys imitate him—like the way he wore his socks or what kind of sneakers he had on. Between the Boys Club and speeches from my parents, I learned to stay away from trouble.

Alvin encouraged me to make the most of my talents. He must have known how my size frustrated me, and he cheered me on as I took on older, bigger opponents. One afternoon we were all outside boxing in a sort of small tournament Alvin had cooked up. The day before, I had heard a kid calling me "pee-wee" behind my back, and I told Alvin to pair us up in the ring. Everybody thought it was a big joke, since this guy was five inches taller and about 30 pounds heavier than me—he was going to *kill* me! But before the match, Alvin showed me how to use my quickness to get in close and then dart away. All through the fight I kept dashing in, throwing a few punches, and then dashing out before he could hit me. After a while he got tired of me hitting him and him chasing me. He lowered his hands, and WHAM, I hit him again. He fell down, and I won the fight. Little did I know that my boxing lessons would come in handy later when I had to dodge elbows thrown my way by the bruisers of pro basketball.

Don't get the wrong idea. As a boxer, I wasn't exactly a

knockout artist. My strength was peppering my opponent with jabs and quick punches, trying to influence the judges by scoring with the more frequent and effective blows.

One bout I particularly remember came during a bona fide tournament in Fort Worth against the Panther Boys Club. The Panther Boys Club was sort of the farm system for Fort Worth's best Golden Gloves fighters. World champions like Donald and Bruce Curry, Steve Cruz, and Gene Hatcher all graduated to the pros from the Fort Worth Golden Gloves team. Fort Worth may have an inferiority complex as far as Dallas, its big brother to the east, is concerned, but not when it comes to boxing.

In one of my tournament fights at Fort Worth, the referee was accusing me of using the inside of my glove—of slapping my opponent and using the laces on his face. I wasn't doing that, but the official kept stopping the bout and signaling with his hand that I was slapping. In my corner between rounds I asked Alvin why the referee insisted I was doing something against the rules when I wasn't. Alvin said my punches were legal and only emphasized that I make sure each and every blow was thrown with the knuckles of the glove. I won the fight. Later that referee told another guy that he didn't think a kid my size had any business being in the ring. Obviously he'd formed an opinion about me from the moment I stepped through the ropes. Putting up with that attitude from my peers was difficult enough. But why did adults have to do the same?

Because I was so tiny I fought in the "beetle-weight" class. There also was a "mosquito-weight," all sorts of categories for little fellas, climbing right up to "flyweight." I won a few fights, lost a few, and enjoyed the competition thoroughly, although I had to admit to myself that I didn't have much future in boxing. There wasn't any "beetle-weight" champion of the world, not that I was aware of.

Turnkey also had a baseball team, the Pirates. I was a pretty good pitcher and shortstop and a decent slap hitter. You can imagine the number of walks I drew, considering the size of my strike zone. And I could get on a pitcher's nerves once I reached base.

I also loved Ping-Pong. At Turnkey we had a table that was a few inches higher than regulation. When my friend, Brian Madlock, and I would play, our heads would barely be even with the table. The first time Alvin ever noticed me, I was playing Ping-Pong. He'd known my parents because he attended their church, St. Mark's Missionary Baptist, but obviously I was easy to overlook. Before long I was his shadow. Every time he turned around, there I'd be, tagging along. Boys Clubs had a camp near Lake Lewisville, north of Dallas. Alvin had to pick up and deliver kids to the camp at various times and I would ride with him. We'd talk about life, about making the right decisions. He was a boxer who'd won the Dallas Golden Gloves middleweight high school title in 1969 and open division middleweight in 1974. He could have turned pro but decided he would come to hate all the negative aspects of the sport. I respected him totally as a man and as an athlete.

Our relationship grew so close that I think some of the other kids became envious. When Alvin would make me captain of a team or announce that I was the starting pitcher, a few guys would gripe, saying, "Alvin must be your daddy." That made me mad. Alvin was my friend and my teacher, but I already *had* a dad. I suppose guys couldn't handle the fact that this little bitty guy could play sports at least as well as them—and in many cases, better.

Alvin would tell me, "Whatever you do in athletics or in life, do it with style, do it with grace. Do it with the feeling in your heart that, 'I can do whatever I set my mind on doing, and don't tell me I can't.'" Sometimes he was loud and boisterous but he had the knack of convincing us he knew the proper way to do things.

Probably the most exciting period of my two-plus years as a Turnkey regular was the 1975 football season. Surprised that I was a football player? So were most of my opponents, especially after I nailed a running back behind the line of scrimmage or caught a touchdown pass. I really took to football.

Alvin coaxed me into joining the Pirates' 12-and-under football team. Football's physical elements didn't scare me. Alvin had boosted my self-confidence. The only problem was outfitting me with equipment: The gear was a bit on the big side, but my oversized helmet and shoulder pads got the job done.

Our first assignment was a practice game against a good team, the West Dallas Boys Club. This was Alvin's rookie year as a football coach and it also was the first experience in organized football for a lot of us kids. Losing that first game left a sour taste. Later I said, "Alvin, I don't want to lose anymore."

He agreed and totally revamped the offense, the defense, the special teams, the positions where many of us were playing. From the first game of the regular season it was apparent that we were a more cohesive unit and knew more about the game than our opponents. We had a lot of spirit. We'd sing psych-up songs on the bus to our games. I wore number 22, a starting wide receiver, safety, and defensive captain. Again, I know it's hard to believe but I was better on defense. I closed fast and hit people with all my strength. Alvin taught me how to set myself into position to deliver a shot. I may have been the smallest guy on the team, but when I tackled an opponent, he knew he'd been taken down. I had a sense for picking up strategy and tried to be Alvin's extension on the field.

Once something was explained to me, you didn't have to tell me again.

We won our first seven games, setting up a season-ending grudge match with, you guessed it, the West Dallas Boys Club. This was a plot line out of a B movie or cheap novel. We were tied with West Dallas for first place in our league. The opposing coach was Cleo High, an excellent football man who had grown up with Alvin. We could tell Alvin was really nervous before the game, at least as jittery as we were. The game was played in enemy territory at Edison High, across the street from the West Dallas Boys Club, and there were quite a few people in the stands. The field looked so enormous that to us it was Texas Stadium. So this was the big time!

We weren't able to generate much on offense, but our defense kept us in the game, getting a safety and holding West Dallas' potent offense to just a touchdown. Still, we trailed, 6–2, and time was running down. Our offense was really dead. I never say much, but I sure wanted this game. When somebody made a mistake or blew an assignment, I'd smack them on the side of the helmet and say, "Wake up, put your head on right, and let's play football." This was serious business.

The game was nearly over before our offense finally began producing. With about 10 seconds to play we had the ball on the West Dallas 4-yard line. Fourth down. Twilight was falling and there were no lights. We figured we had time for one more play: 42 dash-right, a running play that had worked for us all year. My job was to line up on the left side and run a post pattern to occupy a defensive back and linebacker. "We should score on this play," all of us agreed during a time-out.

But I had a funny feeling as the snap count started. When the ball was hiked, I peeled off toward the backfield. Sure enough, their linebacker hadn't taken the bait. He

was waiting in that 4-hole for our running back, Sammy
Gibson. Somehow I reached the hole before Sammy, dove
in, and bumped the linebacker to clear a path. Sammy
hotfooted it into the end zone. The gun sounded. We had
won the game and the championship. We had beaten our
nemesis to win the title. And the littlest guy made the key
block.

You should have seen the celebration; jumping on one
another, rolling around on the ground. You'd think we'd
won the Super Bowl. Alvin gave us a banquet and we all
received trophies. Later we found out Alvin paid for much
of it out of his own pocket.

When football season was over, I finally found time for
basketball. Alvin had played a lot and he taught us everything he knew. Right from the start I found I was able to
use my quickness to steal the ball. I'd come up behind a
guy who was dribbling carelessly and flick the ball out of
his hands. Also, I found out I could jump higher than kids
several inches taller than me. I wore a huge Afro and I
must have been a sight, my hair bouncing in every direction as I brought the ball upcourt.

Although I enjoyed playing other sports, I settled upon
basketball as my primary interest. And once I started
playing for my school teams, I stopped hanging out at
Turnkey. As close as I had been to Alvin for those two
years of my life, we went our separate ways. I didn't see
him again for 12 years.

In February 1987 I was a speaker at a citywide Dallas
Boys Club banquet at Texas Stadium. As I stood in the
parking lot, talking to a group of kids and signing autographs, a man put his hand on my shoulder. I wheeled
around and recognized Alvin. We hugged and I think I
kissed him. At least that's what I remembered later because I said I did during my speech. I talked about Alvin

and how much he and Turnkey had meant to my development as an athlete and a person.

Alvin will always remain one of the most unforgettable characters I know. He's 38 now, and I hear he's thinking of making a comeback in the Golden Gloves. That's Alvin! Never give in. I just thank God Alvin was sent to me at such a formative period in my life.

3

"Now Take This Ball and Put It Through That Hoop"

By the time I was 12, I felt I was good at several sports. But in the course of my exposure to all the athletics at Turnkey, basketball was becoming most important to me. It must have seemed like a strange passion for a kid who was only 4'9" tall and weighed only 90 pounds. I was so little that Charles Lewis (the other shrimp) and I used to play one-on-one games *inside* my garage! We put a hoop up against the back wall, and when it was raining we'd have games in there until we were so sweaty from the humidity we had to quit. Believe me, a gym is much nicer, but at this point I was determined to play seventh-grade basketball and I didn't care *where* I practiced!

Any 12-year-old can get a physical and go out for the team in junior high, but that doesn't mean he'll get to play. The day of tryouts for my seventh-grade team I went over to the gym at Kennedy Curry Junior High with Dextor Dabney, an old friend from my West Dallas days who was the quarterback of our football team and a fellow Boys

Club member. We got in the lay-up lines and started shooting as the coach, Jimmy Tubbs, looked on. I made two lay-ups and was told to sit in the stands while the bigger, "serious" players took practice. It was humiliating sitting there. A lot of the passed-over players left, but I stayed around, hoping I might get another shot.

My friends told me I was getting a raw deal, and I couldn't understand why Coach Tubbs didn't see in me the same things that Alvin saw. Still, I was determined to stick with it, and I kept showing up at team practices just in case they needed me to scrimmage. I think I played a total of about three minutes in six practices. Meanwhile, after practice, I was playing on my own in the neighborhood, sometimes against Bean and Stephanie in our backyard.

The day before the first game I got my break. Quite a few of the guys who were supposed to play had taken the $5 their parents have given them for the physical and spent it on the movies. The rules said you had to have a physical to play (and you can be sure I'd gotten mine). Coach Tubbs, who later became head coach at Kimball High School in Dallas, had no other choice but to put me in the lineup. We played Corsicana, and both Dextor and I scored 20 points in leading us to a win. We never left the lineup after that.

Junior high basketball was some of the most fun I've ever had. You get all excited before every game, thinking that it's the NBA finals. But it isn't, and you know that, too. The pressure isn't there because you're so young and nobody expects anything of you.

In some ways, I think being small was an asset early on, because I was comfortable with my body, while the bigger, ganglier kids were still growing like weeds and as a result were very uncoordinated. I used to dribble around them like a wild man, and Dextor and I thought we were the most potent scoring combination in junior high basketball history. Our team won almost every game, and basketball was giving me new-found happiness and a sense of importance.

The next year, when I was in the eighth grade, we continued our winning ways, marking up victories in all but our very last game. At this point, I was having great fun playing ball, but I had also discovered women. This was, of course, more or less a spectator sport. As a shy teenager my main activities were:

1. Going to the Shamrock roller-skating rink on weekends to skate and look at girls.
2. Being a lookout while Charles kissed Carla Johnson, a girl who lived down the block.
3. Playing basketball.

One night in the spring of 1977, Dr. J changed my priorities.

My brother Bean and I were watching the Philadelphia 76ers play Portland in a critical playoff game. We could not believe what we were seeing: Here was this man, this graceful gazelle of a basketball player, taking complete control of a game in such a way that the other players were reduced to watching, just as we were. Early on, it became obvious that Portland didn't have a chance, but no fan would have considered leaving the game. What we were all witnessing was an athletic genius at work, creating plays, inventing shots that had never been made before. Dr. J wasn't playing, he was *teaching,* and I became his willing pupil.

Dr. J had height, power, and skill. But it was his magic that touched me. As soon as the game ended, I leapt off the couch to see what magical elements I had inside of *me.*

Flying off in the darkness of my backyard toward a rickety wooden backboard with the rim no more than six feet off the ground, I labored to duplicate the heroics I had just witnessed. The drifting arc of his jumpshot, the twisting slam of his majestic dunks—I meant to have these for myself. I stayed out there deep into the night, and the next morning I resolved to keep doing it again and again.

There's a tingle every kid feels walking through the doors of his or her high school for the first time. As torn up and unimpressive as Wilmer Hutchins High may have been from the outside, it represented a bold new challenge for me: I was determined to wear the powder-blue and white jersey of the Wilmer Hutchins Eagles varsity basketball team. Of course, I had to make the freshman team first.

Like most schools, we had two freshman teams—the one that had all the promising star players and the other, which was made up of the misfits. Guess who was a misfit. From the very first practice I knew what was happening: Here I was again, being discounted because of my size. It could have been really depressing, except that Coach Cooper didn't treat us like losers. He was out to win. We did okay, and at least I was the "leader of the unwanted," scoring most of our points. The "other" team, the first team, looked invincible, and they stomped every opponent they faced. I remember coming home one day to my family and telling them how badly I wanted to play with the best players. As always, Janice was there to give some sisterly advice.

"Keep working, Spud," she said. "You'll get your chance. But little guys like you have to try extra hard to prove yourselves. In your heart you know you're a winner, so do your best for your team now, and next year they'll see what they were missing."

It's now my sophomore year, and 13 of us are sitting on the gym floor, listening to Coach Harvey Smith give us his version of a Knute Rockne speech before our first junior varsity game.

"I ain't gonna baby you," he began. "If you're not here to play, fine. We'll leave your ass in the parking lot. If you'll look around, you'll see we've got some players this year, and if we decide it right now, nobody's gonna beat us. I say we open up a big ol' can of ass whoopin' and go get 'em!"

Harvey was the brother of the Wilmer Hutchins head coach, Homer Smith. Neither Harvey nor Homer struck me as having the finest mind in the game. Fortunately for Harvey, however, he had one thing going for him that made him a great coach: his team had so much talent that it couldn't possibly lose. We didn't just beat every team in the district, we *smeared* them. Thirteen heaping helpings from Coach Smith's can of ass whoopin' went a long way.

Later that spring we were working out in the gym, keeping loose and looking toward the varsity, the dream of every kid in the neighborhood. I had just finished a good season, improving my passing and scoring, and was inspired to stay late and keep working on my game. This particular day it was gray and windy, and as we were finishing a scrimmage I noticed the patter of rain upon the huge plastic skylights set in the gym's roof. Soon there was a tremendous swirling, and the wind whipped through the open windows of our locker room, slamming the brown metal locker doors with incredible force. There was a strange whistling sound outside, and we looked at each other with wide, wondering eyes—what was going on?

Suddenly the entire building began to shake. Walking back onto the gym floor, I looked up just as the plastic

27

skylights were ripped from the roof. Rain poured through, and the large paper letters that spelled out CHILDREN ARE THE FUTURE across the side of the gym came loose from the wall and flew off in all directions. Outside, the wind was really picking up now, and we all raced to escape the havoc, leaping into cars or speeding off on bicycles. A moment after we got beyond the school grounds, the tornado appeared, slashing through tree lines and fields and hurtling toward the gym, where it arrived with a crash. The tornado ripped the entire roof off the gym, sending pieces of it everywhere and toppling the baskets. The retractable bleachers were pulled out and twisted, as if mocking spectators to come watch the destruction.

When we returned the next day, the gym was in shambles and the rest of the school had been devastated by the fierce winds. Everything was wet and battered, and the school administrators quickly pronounced the place unusable. The storm had ended our school year a couple of weeks early and had sealed the fate of the old high school. Though we would never get to enjoy it, a new high school was planned for a hilltop two miles away. My class would have to come back to this ramshackle structure, which was patched together by the following fall. It's now a junior high school, but the scars from the storm remain.

Half of high school was over, and I had done pretty well for a guy who was just inching past the five-foot mark. I was also doing pretty well with the books, which made things easier. I've always enjoyed learning, and in the next year I would learn some lessons that would last me the rest of my life. But I did not realize that the storm I had just witnessed was a foreshadowing of things to come: The lessons would be hard and painful.

4

Lessons Learned, Points Made

I'm 16. It's a rainy, late summer afternoon in South Dallas, and inside the Crest Theater, Bruce Lee is karate-chopping his way through half a dozen dull-faced mob goons. Fifteen minutes later, Bruce has cleaned house and he's looking around for the next challenge. One of his kung-fu buddies comes by and tells him that the guys he just sliced, diced, and julienned were cake compared to the ultrabad Ninjas who stole Bruce's chick. No question 'bout it, Bruce has to get his mind right and show these dudes once and for all: no one messes with Bruce's turf.

Varsity tryouts were coming up and I knew I was going to have to perform some basektball-fu on the Wilmer Hutchins High School court. When I wasn't working down at the Soul Mart, I'd been spending every summer day at the Highland Hills recreation center gym, playing hoops with guys in the neighborhood. Those games can get pretty rough, and I was out to prove that I was prepared for varsity ball. Playing reckless, playing with abandon, the message I was sending out was clear: No one messes with this rough, tough, 5'2" hoop-rattling king of the court.

Okay, so maybe no one was really afraid of me, but I did play hard and everyone assured me that I would make the varsity. I even had the endorsement of Mr. Basketball himself, Mookie Smith.

Around Wilmer Hutchins, Mookie was The Man. Brought up to the varsity as a sophomore, Mookie was a clever finesse player who studied the game and had the skills to make the most of what he knew. At 6'1" he was also a great leaper, able to spring up and jam it inside when he wasn't dropping in rainbows from outside.

And Mookie was funny. He still is one of the funniest guys I know. He's got a round face with a devilish smile and he's just smart enough to be dangerous. We grew up together in The Projects, and his family moved South shortly after we did. Even though Mookie was two years older than I, we always played ball together and I learned a lot from him. Many times when we'd try to get in a pickup game with some of the older guys, no one would choose me. But Mookie stood by me, and said he wouldn't play unless I was on his team. We worked a lot on our passing, making up special plays between the two of us, and when we were on the court together you couldn't stop us.

Mookie had carried the Wilmer Hutchins program for two years—the team won over 20 games and captured the district title with ease—before heading to Navarro Junior College. That's where he was when I called him for some encouragement for the varsity tryouts.

"You know Coach Smith better than I do, Mook," I asked, "What's it gonna take?"

"You got the moves, the quickness and the D [meaning defense]," he answered. "But to make varsity, you'll have to use your lips."

"My what?" I asked.

"Your lips, Spud," he shot back. "To kiss the man's ass."

I suspected Homer Smith of playing favorites. He liked his players to come around his office, share their problems, talk about what was happening around the school. He was a burly six-footer, with a moustache so thin you might think he had forgotten to shave. His own basketball-playing days had ended when he was 17 years old. He was an unlikely figure to manage the wealth of talent that the neighborhoods around Wilmer Hutchins provided him. However, some said the talent pool was so deep that the team could win district every year—even without a coach. Being the quiet type, I never bothered to play the political games; I figured if I played the best basketball, I'd see plenty of playing time during the season.

It was Jersey Day, when all the varsity hopefuls turn out as varsity assignments are made and numbers are picked. I planned to ask for number 6, which was Dr. J's number. From his office Smith could see that we all had left the locker room and were assembled in the gym, so he picked up his clipboard and walked out onto the floor. "Grab some wood, boys. I've got some things to say about this year's team."

I fidgeted with a nearly broken shoelace and listened while Smith delivered his yearly exhortation of how the Eagles "would soar to victory" again this year with all the great players he had in front of him. Also included was what players called The Smear, where the chubby coach would brazenly criticize former players—for instance, this time: "I'm glad that Mookie Smith is gone because he was really nothing but trouble. Now take Greg Cunningham here [he pointed proudly to Greg], I know he's gonna run our offense better than that showboat Mookie, and take us farther after we win district. Let's not even think about those hotdogs who are gone. We've got the real winners *right here.*"

I wondered what Smith might say about me after *I* was gone, but I quickly abandoned that thought when Smith finished his speech and pulled out a list of names.

"These are the players who will be on the varsity for the upcoming season," he announced, and began reading. One by one, the 13 names were called and the faces with the names lit up in smiles. My name was not called.

"Is that all?" someone asked.

"Yep," Coach Smith replied. "The rest of you will play on junior varsity this year, and I know you'll do a fine job. Now you varsity players, head down to the far end of the gym and get ready for our first practice. JV players, you'll go with Coach Smith."

Only a few players moved. The rest just stared at me, because my face must have looked as though it was about to explode. My whole body quivered in shock and fury.

"I don't believe he's doing this!" I shouted, and I meant it. I was an athlete and I had *earned* the right to play— earned it through endless hours of practice, giving more and more each time so I would be worthy of that varsity jersey. How many thousands of shots had I taken, how many miles had I run? And this man had the audacity to tell me that after all my work my prize would be denied? He was *stealing* from me!

I had to face Smith alone and hear his explanation. I stormed behind him into his office and slammed the door. "Are you telling me that I'm not on varsity?" I demanded.

"Now sit down, Spud." Smith looked uneasy, and I could tell he hadn't expected so much emotion from me. "You need time to develop. JV is the place. And hey, I'm making you captain of the JV."

I stormed away, and on my way out of the gym all I

could think was, "I can play varsity. You know it, all these other guys know it. I played against them all summer long. This ain't right!"

I never really knew why Smith passed me over—he told me he wanted to play the seniors—this was their last chance at a college scholarship. Later I was told that Smith had heard the taunts of some fellow coaches and the matter of me playing was settled long before the list of players was announced. "You're not going to play that midget, are you, Homer?" they laughed. "You put that spindly little thing out on the floor and someone's going to squash him like a bug. You'll be a fool!" I guess Homer Smith had determined one thing: He was not going to be a fool.

Meanwhile, my teenage world was crumbling. I ran out of the gym and headed to the classroom where my sister Renee was teaching speech and drama class. Without a thought to the students, I threw open the door and marched to the rear of the room. The room went silent for a moment. When Renee recovered from the surprise, she rapidly organized her students into study groups. Her class was studying Shakespeare that day, but now she appeared to have a real-life drama on her hands. I was so angry that my mood must have overwhelmed the whole room.

"What is wrong with you, Spud?" she half whispered, putting her arm around me.

I pulled away and yelled something that even *I* couldn't believe I was saying. "I'm quitting! Coach Smith put me on JV, but forget it! I'll transfer if I have to, but there's no way I'm playing JV. No way!"

"Now hold on, Spud," Renee said. "You mean you're really not on varsity?" As she said it, I could see heads look up from the drama groups. Furious whispering began.

"That's right. He said he wanted me to be captain of the

JV team, that I needed time 'to develop'. I told him I was quitting, so it doesn't matter."

Renee looked me in the eye and said, "Now stop talking crazy, Spud. You love basketball and you're not a quitter. We don't quit in this family. We'll talk to Coach Smith and work this out." Then she agreed to give me a ride home so I wouldn't have to ride the bus and have all those kids asking me questions.

Now I know what you're thinking: Why all the fuss over not making varsity? Aren't there thousands of kids who try out all over America for their high school teams and never make it?

Well, yes, that's true. But after all those hours of relentless practicing, I knew I deserved to make it, and that I was on my way to becoming not just a good ball player, but a great one. I could even play in the NBA! I had begun to dream of basketball glory. Lots of kids dream of becoming a success, but in *my* mind I had made an all-consuming commitment to do whatever it took to attain my dream. Now, after working out every day over the summer, impressing even the *college* guys, giving up dates with girls, a chance for a good job, and parties with my friends, my reward was playing with the younger guys on JV? It just didn't make sense. Even though I didn't play up to the coach, I thought he would understand that I was shy and kept to myself—when it came to playing ball, I was a *doer*, not a talker.

I don't know what I would have done that night without my family. They knew I was down and they all came over to the house to talk to me. Both parents were gone—Dad keeping the store open late, Mom working her maintenance job—so my brothers and sisters lent their own advice.

Janice, the oldest, echoed my sister Renee's feelings.

"Spud, you're no quitter 'cause quitters never win," she said. "Lots of people are talking to Coach Smith right now so maybe there's some hope, but right now the JV is what you have. You know you're the best player on either team, so just go out there and show Smith what a fool he was for passing you up."

"That's right, Spud," said Bean. "This could be a real chance, man. Play on that team and show everybody what you can do."

My third sister, Stephanie, is probably my most fiercely loyal fan and she's not afraid to express her opinion to anybody. When we were growing up she was my one-on-one partner, and we used to run up and down the halls, "dunking" nerf balls through wire hoops we had made from coat hangers and hung on doors all over the house. Now Stephanie was almost as mad as I was.

"Homer Smith is no-count," she began. "He knows how to eat and where to pick up his check each Friday, that's it. Spud, if you're on JV then that's just another good reason why we need a new coach!"

The family's support made me feel loved and I appreciated their encouragement. Every kid needs that. But there was still a gnawing feeling inside me: How would I ever play in the NBA if I couldn't even make my own high school team? I decided to be alone, so I slipped on my running shoes and headed out into the cool September night.

About four blocks from home I broke into a slow jog. I heard the laughter of the kids in the neighborhood as they played in the front yard, and I noticed my figure cast a long shadow in the moonlight, a shadow absorbed in the dusty windows of cars too-long abandoned on the street. I turned north toward the rolling hills behind Bishop College, hills I had trained on to build the strength in my legs. I loved running up those hills, and I especially loved the feeling I got when I reached the top; it was as if I had conquered something greater than myself. I needed to feel that now.

Once on top of the highest hill, I sat alone and gazed out over my town. Through the smoky glow of a nearby streetlight I could see the white frame church on Nandina Street where I had spoken with Reverend Jenkins, a longtime family friend, earlier that day. I remembered the Reverend's words, spoken so earnestly that I felt foolish for wanting to quit: "Be careful, boy," he had said. "The Devil will try to get in you and make you give up your goals. You've got to pray, Spud, and don't give up on your dreams. Even when life seems unfair, keep believing in yourself and God will take care of you."

Keep believing in yourself. That's what I've got to do, I thought. But I knew it would be hard, because the kids at school will see this as a failure. For an entire year, I would be a second-class player as a member of the JV. Smith had humiliated me, and I guess I felt I had suffered enough of that already in my life. Didn't God want me to be a success?

You've got to pray, Spud. Under the night sky, I bowed my head. "Dear Lord, I'm sorry for getting so mad and acting mean to my friends and my family. I don't want to be mean. I just want to play basketball and I guess I wanted to play for the varsity pretty bad. Even though Coach Smith and some others don't believe in me, I know you do and I'm thankful. You made me small and I know you've given me some special talents and I hope to use them right. I'm grateful for everything you do for me, and for watching over me. Amen."

Our first game was against Ennis, and "the gang of misfits" won by 70 points. We were all sky high and I scored

36 points in what I'm sure was the most lopsided game I ever played in. Those poor country boys from Ennis never had a chance.

Looking back, I have to admit that my junior year was really a lot of fun. Three of my best friends, Charles Lewis, Derrick Leonard, and Jeff Linnear, were on the team and we were winning like crazy. Homer Smith's brother Harvey was again the coach and he let us play, or should I say, he let the top six or seven players play, most times without set plays or strategy sessions. Some teams needed more discipline, but I think most players, especially in the professional ranks, will tell you they prefer that let-'em-play style of coaching.

We certainly weren't pros, but we went through the season feeling pretty cocky, and I did extract a little revenge at the expense of one rival coach, Clayton Brooks of South Garland High School. Brooks made no secret of the fact that he thought Spud Webb had no business being in a high school uniform. The kid was a runt, an embarrassment. Well, it just so happened that our first district game was against South Garland on their home court. We came out smoking and "the runt" had racked up 20 points in the first half. In the second half, the South Garland coach assigned two guys to go after me and they both fouled out after sending me to the line 15 times. The Embarrassment somehow managed to score 45 points in all, and we whipped South Garland, 102–51.

We ended the year 23–2, and I led the scoring with 23 points per game average. We won district for junior varsity, while our varsity team struggled. They were losing a lot, and for the first time since anyone could remember, the JV games had drawn crowds almost as big as the varsity. After four straight years of winning district, the varsity fell short. My sister Stephanie, the self-appointed, unofficial spokesperson for the Webb family, took care of the "I-told-you-so's" around the neighborhood while I kept my mouth shut. One thing I learned: It's always better to do your talking on the court, letting your play speak for you. Besides, I had learned a good lesson about humility, and I think Homer Smith learned his lesson, too: Never underestimate a little man with a big heart.

5

The Art of Jumping

See if you can pick out which of the following is the Official Most Asked Question of Spud Webb:

1. Spud, are you engaged to Whitney Houston, Janet Jackson, or both?

2. Spud, how often do you and Ted Turner meet to discuss market strategies in the cable television industry?

3. Mr. Webb, have you ever had dinner with Wilt Chamberlain, Kareem Abdul-Jabbar, and Bill Walton at the same time, and if so, did you order shrimp?

4. Say, man, how do you jump so high?

It's a tough choice, but the answer is number four. Everybody wants to know how a little guy like me can dunk a basketball and block shots, things that allow me to play basketball with the big guys. Well, listen up.

First of all, a lot of my talent is God-given, and there's no substitute for that. But I know that everyone has potential to increase their vertical jump, some with dramatic results. To be a great leaper, you first have to understand what jumping is all about.

The key to jumping is leg strength, which anyone can

improve. Good jumpers usually have larger, stronger thighs, with smaller calves. Calf muscles have very little to do with jumping motion, and should be kept as loose and limber as possible—*not* tight. A good leap occurs when the athlete firmly plants his foot (or even both feet) and takes a short dip downward, which doctors call a flexion. You don't want to squat down too far or you kill your spring. Squatting too low with too much bend in the knee is a common mistake for most young players.

Now that you've flexed, you begin to throw all your weight upward, using your arms, head, everything—imagine yourself as a rocket being launched into space. Interestingly enough, once you're off the ground there is very little you can do to change the jump. You're on a preset course and you might as well sit back and enjoy the ride.

Between my junior and senior year, I set out on a training program that, although I wasn't aware of it at the time, was almost a perfect regimen for improving my leaping ability. Even though I had enjoyed a successful JV season, I wanted to be in top shape for varsity ball, so I spent my spring and summer working on every aspect of my game. A big part of that was jumping.

To begin with, I started running religiously. My friend Mookie was back in town, and every morning we would get up and run the hills around our neighborhood. Running uphill was much harder, but it made our knees and thighs stronger, while keeping our ankles flexible. When I wasn't running hills, I ran stands at the football field or even inside at the gym. Anyone who's ever gotten on one of the stair machines at a fitness club knows how hard running up steps can be.

All this running kept me skinny, and obviously, the leaner you are, the less weight you have to carry with you when you jump. But leaping isn't necessarily a function of weight; it's more related to your body fat. For example, Charles Barkley of the Philadelphia 76ers, sometimes known as the "Round Mound of Rebound" is a whopping 6'6", 260 pounds, but he can jump into space. Yet while the average man has around 18 percent body fat, Charles only carries about 9 percent. All my teammates on the Atlanta Hawks are really lean, and we're probably the best jumping team in basketball. So, eat right and keep your weight down.

Flexibility is really important, and I've always done lots of stretching. Basketball is so demanding on your body— forcing you to change directions at high speeds, to reach out and grab balls thrown away from you, and so forth— that you need to concentrate on becoming as limber as possible. One good exercise for keeping your calves flexible is simply standing flat-footed on the floor and slowly raising the front of your foot toward the shin while your heels stay flat.

Finally, the best exercise you can do for jumping *is* jumping. I didn't walk out onto a court one day and decide to dunk a basketball, I practiced it day after day after day. After playing ball for two or three hours, we would line up in the gym in what we called "punchlines." Translation: "Let's line it up boys, and see who can punch it [dunk it]." That meant dragging your tired butt onto the court and jumping as high as you possibly could time after time. In any given week, I probably tried to dunk at least 100 times. Another good exercise is to take a basketball and jump while bouncing the ball off the backboard, catching the ball in your fingertips and tipping it back up on the board at the top of your jump. This not only helps your jumping, but it's also good practice for *timing* your jump. I've seen lots of guys who could jump like kangaroos, but they didn't know *when* to jump. By the way, they used to teach you that wearing ankle weights or weighted vests was a good training technique, but no longer: These weights put too much strain on your knees and ankles.

If you want to chart your progress on how high you jump, you can use the same test used at major colleges to measure vertical leap. It's very simple. Get a standard ink pad and press your fingertip in it to get it good and black (you guys who have been busted should have no problem with this). Then stand next to a wall (not *inside* your house or your mom will throw a fit!) and reach as high as you can from a standing position with both feet flat on the ground. Don't cheat! Touch your finger to the wall and you've got your vertical reach. Now, re-ink your finger and go back to the same spot. This time, jump as high as you can and touch the wall at the top of your leap. The difference between the two dots is your vertical leap. They say top athletes can usually jump one-third their height, which is 20 inches for a person 5' tall, 24 inches for someone 6' tall. Me? I jump 42 inches, which is two-thirds of my height. That figure may be higher now—I've been practicing some more.

By the way, don't think that jumping is just a black thing. Look around professional sports and you'll see many white athletes who have superb leaping ability. High jumpers, volleyball players, and yes, even a few basketball players can get up pretty well. Like me, most of these guys have worked to improve their leaping ability in addition to what the good Lord gave them.

For those of you who seem forever bound to earth by excessive amounts of gravity, don't worry. As any coach will tell you, jumping ability is in no way crucial to good basketball. In fact, all the coaches I've ever had told me to keep my feet on the floor. Jumping ability is simply an asset, like long arms or big hands. Thinking ability is much more important, and sometimes while the guy who is guarding you is flapping around in the air, you can be dribbling right under him for an open shot. And remember: What goes up, must come down. Landing properly is essential, because there are so many injuries caused by players coming down wildly, without their feet squarely underneath them. You can't be stiff, either; your knees have got to be ready to absorb the shock when you land, especially if you bounce off someone on the way down.

So why do so many NBA stars keep leaving the floor, playing above the rim? Because it's fun. The game is altogether different when you're flying high, and those athletes who can do it will keep taking off because they yearn for that feeling of being in the air, floating above the other players. It's a magical, spiritual feeling when you're out in front on the fast break, streaking to the bucket . . . you get the pass and you see the basket looming ahead, waiting for you . . . you have your target, you're locked in, and it's as if nothing can stop what is about to happen . . . you plant your foot and suddenly you're soaring, rising higher and higher toward your goal . . . reaching out your arm, you extend the ball to the basket, like some offering to be placed on a high altar . . . but then you realize you're flying, that you're above this rim and you've defied the force which holds you down . . . it's a celebration, a sense of joy and power and now, at the very peak of your flight you deliver the ball to the hoop, sending it with all the force you possess, and you wait for the sound . . . it's the roar of the crowd with all eyes focused on *you* as you soar and send your message with a thunderous thunk . . . you land and your body springs back up, and the thrill of the moment rises up inside you.

Back in high school a number of my friends dunked with ease. But I was the smallest figure on the floor; how I longed to feel that feeling! Every afternoon I would try, and each time the basket was just as impossible to reach.

But I kept at it, and somehow I knew that if I could just reach over that rim to dunk, all my dreams of basketball glory might come true.

It was a summer I will never forget. Each morning, Mookie and I were up with the sun, running the hills or the bleachers, depending on the weather. Then we hit the weight room, and I tried to add muscle to the 110-pound frame I carried. Sometimes we ate lunch, and sometimes we played right through lunch, an endless series of one-on-one games that will probably continue until one of us dies. Each day we spent at least an hour philosophizing, as teenagers are apt to do. We made it a practice to break to watch *Sanford and Son* and *Good Times* on TV. Then it was back to the gym from 5 to 8 P.M. for games and the punchline. I'd come home, grab some dinner, and on many nights, I'd put flashlights in the trees so I could see to shoot well into the night. Finally, after my mom yelled at me to cut out the racket, I'd be in bed, dreaming of the day I made it big.

Even though I'm still a little bitter about it, I see now why I needed that season on junior varsity. First, I learned not to take anything for granted, and ever since that time I've worked as hard as I could to improve my chances of achieving my goals. Second, I found that I loved the game of basketball more than I cared about the relative prestige of whatever team I was playing on, but I also knew that, if possible, I wanted to play this game somehow, some way in the professional ranks. Finally, it reaffirmed for me that God has a plan for my life, and that His plan isn't always exactly what I wanted it to be; however, if I would just be patient, God would show me what direction to take and help me to get there. That has become a key for my life—letting go and letting God run the show.

6

The Littlest Eagle

When I grew up, there was no such thing as a sauna in South Dallas, unless you counted the Highland Hills gym when the air conditioning went out. The Texas heat did not dissuade us from playing, mind you, and on one special August afternoon the boys in the punchline were having trouble holding on to their sweat-soaked basketballs —pumpkins were flying all over the place.

When it came my turn to dunk, I held on with both hands. Unable to palm a ball with one hand, using both made it easier and I needed every advantage if I was to finally zoom high enough to score my first jam. On this particular try—who knows, maybe the 1,238th time I had attempted to dunk—I felt a sudden surge of energy, an unexplainable extra lift as I shot toward the hoop. There, with my friends around me, dripping from the heat of that room, I hung above the rim for an instant and pushed the ball through—a slam dunk!

There were some big smiles, some small applause. As I got back in line, a couple of my buddies gave me a wink.

" 'Bout time," they grinned.

I was a member of the club.

That first dunk was a major step for me, and with achievement came confidence. I had climbed something like three and a half feet through space to put a ball through a hoop and, by doing so, eliminate in my mind the obstacle of height. Now, when people would look at me and remark, "Wow, he's so short!" there was an emphatic reply: "Yeah, but he can *dunk!*" Suddenly I had given people a reason to accept me on a basketball court (even though, in years to come, my ability to dunk would have very little to do with my overall success as a player). More importantly, I had set a goal that was quite literally out of reach—and reached it! Upon such humble beginnings are careers made.

Greg Cunningham said it was the shortest tryout in history. Greg was All-Everything at Wilmer Hutchins, a great football player and one of the only juniors to make varsity the year before. He was alongside Coach Smith during our first practice when yours truly got underneath his man and stole the ball, breaking the other way toward the basket. Adrenaline flowing, I left earth somewhere around the free-throw line and finished just above the basket, where I pounded in a fairly respectable dunk. If Darrell Dawkins had been there to name it, he might have called it a "Five-Foot-Two Wearin' Powder Blue, Smith Shocked, Gym Rocked, High Flyin', Varsity Buyin' Slam-Bam-Thank-You Jam."

Smith's mouth was wide open. He looked at his brother, and *his* mouth was wide open.

"What do you think, Coach?" grinned Cunningham.

"I think Spud just made the varsity," he replied, shaking his head. "And I think there are some people in this district who are in for a surprise."

Ask almost any NBA player about his happiest basketball days and he'll probably tell you stories of his senior year in high school. High school is the last year you play just for the fun of it, with relatively little pressure whether you win or lose. In high school, the coach can't yell at you too much, because you're just a kid; the cute-looking cheerleader is someone you date, not some gymnast who's on scholarship; and after a big win, the team boosters (usually your friend's parents) can take you out to Burger King to celebrate without worrying about violating NCAA rules. The only problem with high school is that you still have to look cool at all times, because there are chicks in the stands and fully one-half of the reason you are doing what you do is to impress *them,* not some pro scouts or corporate marketing executives. This is a very important point because high school is also the last year of your life that you can get away with all sorts of "cool" tricks to impress women—they'll fall for the walk, the haircut, the way you get up in anguish after barely bumping into some opponent and keep playing—all that stuff. The minute you get to college, forget it. College chicks have figured all that stuff out. For example, in high school it is absolutely mandatory that after you blow a wide open, easy lay-up, you throw a temper tantrum. Point to anyone within 10 feet and claim they fouled you. Point to the line painted on the floor and insist the stripe is too thick and you tripped on it. Point to the shoddy lighting in the gym ceiling and say the glare off the backboard blinded you. But never ever admit it was your fault, because there are chicks present and you ain't gonna get an after-game kiss if they think you are the type who chokes open lay-ups.

In college, it's a different story. Before you can even think of an excuse, the women are shouting, "Can you believe that chump missed a *lay-up?*" So you just shrug your shoulders and run back down the court. Besides, you know you're not going to get away with anything in college anyway, because suddenly there is a terrible new presence in your life: Sportswriters.

Let's get back to high school and the fortunes of our favorite squad of roundballers, the Wilmer Hutchins Eagles. Even though they were destined to have a great year, the boys in blue and white did not start off too well.

Our first game of the season was against Kimball High School, and their new coach was none other than my old seventh and eighth grade coach, Jimmy Tubbs. I'll never forget him because for the first year I played for him, he had misunderstood my name and kept calling me "Fudge." We'd be in a crucial situation, and huddled over on the sideline, Tubbs would look at us and say, "We got to get the ball to Fudge, boys. Ol' Fudge has the hot hand." And everybody would look at each other and think, "Should we tell him?"

Well, we lost to Coach Tubbs, but Fudge scored 24 points in his first varsity game and felt pretty good about it. We lost another close one, then beat Pinkston High for our first win. I was waterbugging in and out, getting fouled like crazy. Fortunately, all those hours of free-throw shooting over the summer paid off and I hit 17 of 19 from the line while scoring 35 points.

Our next game was against Dunbar High in Fort Worth, and you might say it was the night Spud Webb was discovered. We were playing at the Wilkerson Grounds across from Texas Christian University, and because Dunbar always has great teams, there was a big crowd there. We were down at the half, 54–41, and so we decided to open things up a bit and get creative. Late in the third quarter, Dunbar's hot-shooting guard, Willie Ashley, came up with a dunk. I got the ball at midcourt, stopped for a second, and then decided to answer back. A quick stutter step, and when I got to the free throw line I went up for a one-handed dunk—and *wham!* The crowd went absolutely crazy and even though we lost by 17 points, everyone was buzzing about this little number 4 from Wilmer who dunked. The next day, sportscaster Dale Hansen from WFAA-TV (Dallas's ABC affiliate) came to our practice and interviewed me.

There's nothing like that first interview. Man, you think you are *the* coolest person on earth, and you freak out when you see yourself on TV. The only thing that brings you down to earth is your brothers and sisters telling you how big your nose looks or how dumb you sound trying to make profound statements about your life when you're only 17 years old. Anyway, it was great fun, and it made my senior year start off with a bang.

One other bit of early fame came after a wild game we played with Carter High School right before Christmas. They had an awesome team that year, with a brother combination, the Wagner twins (who both later played at Centenary) and Ron Singleton, who went on to play at Arizona State. They were picked to win the city, and I was really pumped up for the game. In the first quarter I had 14 points, which is pretty good for high school, and we led all the way into the fourth quarter. With less than five minutes to go, Roger Wagner went crazy, pouring in seven straight baskets, and they nipped us, 106–105. I had scored 39 points and played my heart out, and several sportswriters approached me after the game. The next day, a big story came out in the *Dallas Morning News,* and Charles Lewis and I went all over town putting quarters in the newsracks and then taking every paper in the machine. We filled up the back of my car, and passed out papers the next day at school. Okay, so sometimes I didn't maintain my cool. . . .

Through the first 10 games of the season, the Eagles looked as though they had their feathers plucked. We were

4–6, and we needed some punch. We got it when football season ended and a top player came over to the hoops squad. With the help of Dextor Dabney, my old chum from The Projects and grade-school days, we started winning like crazy, especially when it came time for district to start.

We had a five-game winning streak going into South Garland, the home of Coach Clayton Brooks, one of my early critics. We were playing on their court, and with six minutes left in the fourth quarter, our team was down by five. Cunningham had carried us most of the way, and now Coach Smith turned to me. "Spud, get us out of here," he said, and then he sat down. That was it. You might say our coach was a man of highly sophisticated coaching technique. Then again, you might not.

Anyway, I started taking the shots, and they started falling. One came off a steal, which I thought about dunking, then played it safe and laid it in. It gave me 12 fourth-quarter points, and we rallied to win a critical game. Afterwards, I saw Coach Brooks and he said a lot of nice things to me, telling me that he wasn't a critic, he was a believer. He proved it, too; unbeknownst to me, Brooks had been college roommates with Midland Junior College head coach Jerry Stone. When it came time for me to visit Midland, I found that Brooks had given Stone a glowing recommendation of me, which meant a lot.

Every high school has a big rival, and for us it was Highland Park High, a rich kid school in the city's ritziest neighborhood. I can't say too much in a negative way about Highland Park, because my co-author, Reid Slaughter, went there and he's still a big fan of the Scots, as they call themselves. When Wilmer Hutchins first moved into the same district as the Scots, everyone thought there would be a big racial thing, since The Hutch is all black and Highland Park is all white, but it never materialized.

The rivalry stemmed from the fact that, somehow, HP always had great basketball teams, even though their school has a small enrollment and all they get is skinny white guys who are rarely bigger than 6'5". They play smart, fast-break basketball, and have excellent coaching. They all look pretty good, too; probably because they're tan from those Hawaiian vacations and playing tennis at Dallas Country Club! On this night, they drove over in their Mercedes Benzes and Jaguars to play the homeboys from South Dallas—it was one heck of a game.

The gym was packed and both sides rocked the stands with foot-stomping and spirited yells. Both teams were undefeated in the district, and while both had potent offenses, the score was tied at the half with relatively few points scored, 29–29. In the second half, we took a slim lead behind Barry Williams's shooting, but the Scots fought back. The lead seesawed several times down to the last few seconds, when one of the HP forwards sank a baseline jumper to tie the score at 69. With less than 30 seconds left, we took a shot and missed, and HP had the ball, heading downcourt when somehow the ball was loose on the floor. Eleven seconds left. Greg Cunningham scooped up the loose ball and called time-out. Time in and four seconds left, the ball comes to me. With an HP player thundering toward me, I took the ball straight in and laid it up just as the buzzer sounded—but the ball would not go in! It rolled around the rim at least seven or eight times, while the crowd stared in anticipation. It was like watching the ball on a Las Vegas roulette wheel, wondering where it will come down, and who will be lucky. Finally it fell through—we had won! The scoreboard flashed "HOME 71, VISITOR 69" and the place went completely nuts. I think we set some new records for hysterics while celebrating that night, with people singing, hugging and kissing each other, throwing food around, and pouring

Cokes on each other's heads. No one wanted to leave the gym that night, especially me. It was a moment every kid dreams of, to sink the winning shot against your arch rival and win not only the game but the affection of your community as well. Back at home that night, my parents told me how proud they were, and all my brothers and sisters hung around the house and made a big deal out of their little brother's basket. More than anything, I loved that family closeness. Fans can be fickle, and friendships can fade, but the unselfish love of your family is what keeps you going, even when those last-second shots *don't* fall in.

I think that one of the reasons I loved the game of basketball so much is that it did bring us closer together as a family. We had always been tight-knit growing up, but as my sisters and brothers got older they left the house and pursued their own lives. Even Dad had slowly but surely moved out of the house, spending so much time with the store that he finally got a place near the Soul Mart to save the long drive home each night. He and Mom had slowly grown apart in the past four years, and even though I was 17, it still bothered me to have him away so much. Dad, the hard-edged minister's son, was a positive influence on me in so many ways; selfishly, I wanted him home.

And tonight, he *was* home. I had made the winning basket, and we were all gathered together. Basketball had given me this moment, and I loved the game even more because of it. All my work, all my long hours of running, lifting weights, shooting hoops from morning to midnight was worth that feeling of unity I felt with both my teammates and my family. I knew then I would do anything to keep playing this game as long as I could.

We had won eight straight games, and if we weren't unbearably cocky and obnoxious *before* (the only thing more self-congratulatory than a high school senior male is one who is given a reason to be), now we were *really* making the most of our success. We took long lunch hours, hanging out in the gym and sometimes getting out on the floor for a one-on-one game that might last, say, through history class. We elevated lollygagging in the halls to an art form, and often spent hours in my sister Renee's classroom, sitting in the back and cracking jokes about kids in her drama classes or anything else that came to mind. Another pastime was descending upon the bake sales and cook-offs that were held to raise money for the Senior Prom at the end of the year. My sister and the other young teachers would cook sausages or barbecue and sell it at school, and their biggest problem was stopping us basketball players from eating up the profits. Most of us made good grades anyway, especially my pal Jeff Linnear, who was always studying, so we got away with murder. In our minds, we ruled the school.

Away from school we had lots of fun without getting into much trouble. Most of my friends came from good families. When we were offered drugs or booze we just said no. I know it's hard for a lot of kids. They see their classmates, friends, maybe even their parents regularly getting bombed. In some places it's easier to buy a joint than a hamburger—more vendors, no waiting. In high school, college, and even in the pros, I've known plenty of people who got off on drugs and booze in a big way. But I always knew it wasn't for me. And once you've said no a few times, people will respect you for it. It gets easier to say no, and people start getting the picture: They stop offering you the stuff after a while.

I remember accidentally taking a sip of beer at a family cookout once. I spat it out—it was the nastiest stuff I'd ever tasted. Someone told me, "Spud, you have to *learn* to like it. Everybody hates it at first." Well, why bother? To me it wasn't worth suffering for. I'll take an ice-cold Coke anytime over that stuff.

Am I strange because I don't drink, don't take drugs? I don't think so. I don't like myself more because I don't do drugs—but I know I'd like myself less if I did.

Sure, sometimes my friends and I got into some mischief, but it never amounted to much. My sister Janice had given me her old Pontiac Firebird to drive, and not many kids had cars back then. It was bright gold and we must have put 25,000 miles on that car, just driving aimlessly around the neighborhood, hanging out and talking trash. One thing about that car was the hubcaps: They were a special kind of spoke wheelcovers, which Janice had special-ordered from the factory, and only two of them had been stolen. Charles Lewis, Derrick Leonard, and I made it a project to find those missing hubcaps, which we convinced ourselves had been stolen by someone in the neighborhood so it was only right that we steal them back. Night after night we cruised the streets, looking for cars that might be wearing those long-lost wheelcovers. Sometimes one of us would see a car that had similar hubcaps on it, and we'd slow down to a crawl and slump way down in our seats so no one could tell we were casing the situation. I was always too scared to get out of the car, so Charles would go, or Derrick would extract his 6'4" body out of my backseat and tiptoe up to the car and check out the wheelcovers. We kept that up all year long, and we never found a single car with the same spoke pattern.

We did "steal" a few movies, though. That is, we discovered a perfect vantage point up on this hill across from the Lone Star Drive-in, where on Monday nights they showed X-rated movies. I don't like to admit this, but I think we watched dirty movies in just about every foreign language there is (by the way, most of the plots are the same). To make a real night of it, we'd go buy popcorn, or stop by WW Grocery and get 10 chicken wings for 99¢, and go up to the hill as soon as it got dark. Then we watched for hours. Charles used to kid me because he'd say, "C'mon, Spud, it's two A.M. and we've got school tomorrow!" But somehow we'd always manage to stay for at least one more.

There were girls at Wilmer Hutchins High School and yes, I did gather up the nerve to ask one of them out. One of them. As I've said, I was really shy as a kid, very quiet, and not exactly Billy Dee Williams when it came to picking up girls. Her name was Sean Shannon, and she was very sweet, so I felt great when she said yes to my first date offer. I remember we went to see *American Gigolo* with Richard Gere and all the guys were talking about what a stud he was in that movie. I tried to pick up some pointers, but when you're shy you generally know what to do . . . you just can't bring yourself to do it.

I've always been shy. You don't have to be a Muhammad Ali, always calling yourself "the greatest," in order to be a good athlete. My mom says I never talked much when I was a baby. In fact, I still don't talk much. In class I almost never raised my hand to volunteer an answer to a teacher's question. That doesn't mean I didn't know the answer, though. I didn't go on as many dates as some of my friends. That doesn't mean I didn't like girls.

What I always preferred to do was *look*. Just see things. Even if I didn't open my mouth much in family conversations I was always watching how people talked. This way I not only heard what they were saying, I could see what they really meant to say. I figure I learned a lot more about people and life by not shooting off my mouth and using that time instead to see what was actually going on.

I think this has helped me in my basketball career, too.

When I push the ball up the court, I see everything. I know where all the opponents are, and where my teammates are, and where they're thinking of going. If there's an opening, I'll see it. I don't know if you can practice seeing, but if so, I've done it.

On the basketball court I always felt comfortable, confident. I don't cut up in the locker room as much as some people do, but once I set foot on the court, I lose all my shyness. I learned early on I loved games with wild finishes and a lot of pressure, when the team would look to me for points. Good thing, because we were involved in quite a few rousing games that year. After the big Highland Park victory, there was a 53–52 thriller over Lakeview, then a 71–70 win over North Garland (I managed to force a turnover with 16 seconds left, and Cunningham canned two free throws to put us ahead).

Then we had a barnburner with Garland High that went into overtime. It was your typical unbelievable game. We came back in the fourth quarter and I sank two free throws to tie the score with less than 20 seconds left and send the game into overtime. Then big, bad Barry Williams hit two free throws with no time left to win it, 72–70. Easy, right?

We finished district with two more tough games, including a three-point win over Highland Park at home in which I had 23 points, 10 in the fourth quarter. Our 13–1 district record made us champions, and we all celebrated the *way* we won it, with so many gutsy, last-minute victories.

We carried our 26–8 season record and a lot of pride into Sprague Field House to face our bidistrict opponent, the Grand Prairie Gophers. It was hard to take anyone named the "Gophers" very seriously, but we wiped the smiles away long enough to beat them by 16 points. I felt great and had a good shooting game, scoring 30 points, and our team was deadly from the free-throw line, hitting 31 of 34 chances.

Our win sent us to the regionals, which meant we got to pile into a bus followed by cheerleaders and a caravan of fans and drive to College Station, where Texas A & M is located. That night, in the G. Rollie White Coliseum, we faced the Longview Lobos, who sported a 6'8" forward named Steffond Johnson. Steffond later went to LSU and now plays for the L.A. Clippers in the NBA, so you know we had plenty to worry about. On our way out of the locker room, someone pointed out that it was Friday the 13th, but the source of our bad luck wasn't the date, or even Steffond, but a kid named Jerry Ragster. We kept it close all the way, but never could take the lead because Ragster was hitting everything he tossed up. He ended up with 39 points, and we ended up with a loss.

Riding back to Dallas, I looked out of the bus as the Texas landscape raced by and wondered what would happen to me. Would this year turn out to be my greatest? I didn't think so. Inside I knew I had a future in basketball, and all the postseason honors I racked up certainly seemed to indicate that I was going places. But where? Even though I had averaged 26 points a game, been named Player of the Year, All-Metro, and All-State, not one major college had contacted me. Do you think the fact that I was 5'4" had something to do with it?

There are two key things every young man needs in his life: One is a comfy couch to lounge on while watching TV and the other is sound motherly advice. Many nights during the Great Where-to-Go-to-College Debate I reclined on one while waiting for the other. Mom did maintenance work for Dallas Power & Light, and she usually got home just after midnight. I always waited up for her because I didn't like the idea of her being downtown that late at night any more than she liked the idea of her tiny son running reckless on a basketball court with men twice his size. We looked out for each other, and still do.

After a few weeks we all stopped hoping that UCLA or UNLV would call and concentrated on my two best (and only) offers, from North Texas State University and Midland Junior College. Mom liked Midland from the beginning because it was smaller and therefore, she reasoned, less physical in the style of play so her baby boy would have less chance of getting hurt. She also thought that Midland would give me a chance to develop more, both athletically and academically. Translation: Out in West Texas, there was nothing to do but study and play basketball.

On the other hand, North Texas State was in Denton, just 35 miles from Dallas, and was a major college that was bucking to gain entrance into the Southwest Conference. Bill Blakeley was NTSU's head coach, and he had built an outstanding basketball program, compiling a record of 135–80 in his seven years there. Bill had been in basketball all his life, playing college ball at Texas A & M and Abilene Christian, then playing semipro ball for two years and coaching at St. Marks High School in Dallas. He also was a coach for the Dallas Chaparrals of the old ABA, so he knew many aspects of the game.

Bill was a wild dresser, a flashy, flamboyant coach who had a knack for finding great talent in unlikely places. Maybe that's how he found me. Bill says he first saw me during a JV game my junior year in high school, and he recruited me enthusiastically my senior year. I was very tempted to take his offer, especially because Mookie was playing at NTSU that year and we both thought it would be great fun to play together. Whenever Mookie and I

were "highsiding"—our term for cutting up, making fun
of things—Mook claimed he taught me everything I know
about basketball. I'd joke back that the only thing he ever
taught me was how to pass the ball—to *him*, that is, so he
could shoot all the time. The chance to play for a major
college with my best friend would have been a dream come
true for both of us, except there was a problem: NTSU
already had two excellent point guards, and Mookie was
the shooting guard. Bill knew I wanted to play, and so in
the end even he suggested I start my career at Midland.

The junior college route would give me a chance to start
immediately, which was very attractive since I was convinced I had the ability to compete with any college player.
I thought I had proven that during the annual High School
Seniors All-Star Game, held in Waco. Every year the place
is full of NCAA Division I coaches, and after the game
each of the players is approached by all the interested
coaches. I talked with a few people, but not one showed
any genuine interest; I was too small to play, they said. I
was *so* frustrated by that. No one looked at how I played,
they only saw my size. I kept thinking that surely with all
these educated, astute judges of basketball talent, someone
will recognize that my smaller size is an *asset,* not a liabil-
ity, making me quicker, more mobile around the court.
Finally, there was one: Jerry Stone of Midland Junior College.

From the beginning, Jerry treated me with respect, at
least as much as any 17-year-old kid deserves. He didn't
make any short jokes or dwell on my liabilities. He told
me I had exceptional talent and would be just the guy to
run his offense in Midland, where they had come off an
outstanding year, winning the Western Conference title.
Furthermore, he had signed Chester Smith, a friend of
mine from Wilmer Hutchins who was very talented, and
that might ease my mind about being away from home. I

knew that nothing would make me any less homesick, but when I visited the Midland campus I was really impressed: They had a huge, almost brand-new gym as nice as any I had ever seen, and a modern, well-equipped campus right in the middle of Oil Boom, U.S.A.

I talked everything over with Bill Blakeley, and he said the scholarship offer from NTSU would still be good the next year, if I wanted to move up my sophomore year. All signs pointed me to Midland, and I signed on. Mookie would have to get his assists from someone else.

The decision was made and the pressure was off. There was some relief in that, although the disappointment remained that I was not going to a major college. One of 10 All-State players out of 5,000 basketballers in Texas and no one wanted me. That hurt. But as my brother Bean said, "Spud, the only folks who really know how good you are are the guys you play against. They know how fast you are, how well you pass and shoot and put pressure on the defense. But Spud, they don't make the rules."

I had to accept that, but I didn't have to accept the "too-small-to-play" label the coaches and scouts put on me. Each day that summer, I worked as hard as I could to improve. Playing in summer leagues with players from colleges all over the country, as well as with local hotshots who never made it to college (these leagues are sponsored by local businesses in Dallas, and have wild, free-form games that are as much fun to watch as any organized college game), I honed my skills, trying to become a complete player, both offensively and defensively.

When I wasn't playing organized ball, I continued playing one-on-one with Mookie. We took turns pretending we were Gus Williams, our mutual hero second only to Dr. J, and we even tied our shoelaces behind our ankles the way Gus did. Gus has those amazing stop-n-go moves that confound almost any defense, and he always has that look of total cool on his face, like a modern-day Walt Frazier. Another hero was Maurice "Mo" Cheeks of the 76ers, because he pushed the ball up the court so fast—something I still emulate today. The rest of the time we spent at Mickey D's (McDonald's), hanging out, talking and philosophizing, solving everyone's problems but our own. For us, playing basketball was half the fun; laughing and joking about what happened while we were playing was the other half.

The summer was over, and in a few days I would be leaving home for the first time. As it is for most kids, that prospect was both frightening and exhilarating. The most important thing was that I would be playing basketball—my devotion, my joy; but I had no idea that the next seven months at this unassuming little college would yield so much high drama, producing a season so unpredictable and heroic that some said it had all been concocted out of a Hollywood script.

7

West Texas Basketball Boom

In September 1981 the price of oil was $34 a barrel, which meant about $32 billion a year for the state of Texas and some pretty good times for your average Midland oilman. And I would soon learn from observing many of the J.R. Ewing types who attended Midland College basketball games that no one knows how to make noise like a Texas oil baron when his wells are pumping and the price is right.

Despite its extraordinary wealth, Midland never dazzled me with its excitement or good looks. Literally out in the middle of nowhere, it was the last place in which I expected to become famous. Yet fame would find me, and the richness of my experience there would more than fill up the geographical emptiness of the place.

Since your life won't be complete until you know more about this exotic spot, I'll give you the 20-second-time-out tour of Midland. First, about 82,000 people live there, although it's probably less than that now because the U.S. oil industry got slam-dunked on by the Arab oil producers. The town got its name because it's halfway between Fort

Worth and El Paso, cities that are only a little more exciting than Midland. Everything in the whole area is flat, including the houses, which are all one-story and so spread out that you need a road map in the mansions to get from one end to the other. Midland is not a very popular place with the brothers, being only about 8 percent black.

Midland College averages around 3,000 students, and at the beginning of my freshman year, eighteen of them wanted to play basketball. Only two were sophomores, Lance McLain and Puntus Wilson. I knew Puntus from his days at South Oak Cliff High School in Dallas, and he was as good a player as there was in junior college. So how good was that? Well, since we're getting educational here, it might be interesting to learn just what junior college basketball is all about.

The junior college ranks are a little like your average jail cell, in that everyone in there thinks they don't belong, or were put there for the wrong reasons. In this case, most players feel they're good enough to be playing major college ball, but because of a bad reputation, poor grades, or an unusual physique (too skinny, too weak in the upper body, or, ahem, too small), they weren't chosen or didn't qualify for a Division I school. The real story is a little different. First of all, it's true that many junior college players can't make Division I because of their grades. But most of these guys are from inner-city high schools that are shining examples of social promotion; if you can play ball, you pass, regardless of how well you read or write. Bill Blakeley used to coach out at a tiny little school called Christian College of the Southwest, and he won several championships because he would go to New York each year and track down brilliant ball players off the city courts who were out of high school but had no chance of passing a college entrance exam. Blakeley set up tutors for the kids, and once they had some decent teaching they flowered into reasonably good students. I don't know if any of those guys ever went on to play Division I, but at least they got a little bit of an education, which is critical, and they experienced that sense of achievement you get from playing on a college court. By the way, in 1985 Texas enacted the "no pass, no play" rule, which said that a high school student must have passing grades in all of his or her courses to be eligible to participate in extracurricular activities such as sports. I think it's a great rule and it should help a lot of young people get the education they need first, before worrying about playing sports.

Academic reasons aside, many players found themselves in junior college ranks because they were renegades, playing a reckless, maverick style of basketball that didn't fit into a particular system. For instance, some schools play a half-court offense that requires players of great patience, who can run several patterned plays and wait for scoring opportunities to open up. Other schools want a purely physical team, with powerful players who can out-muscle opponents. Still others are fast-break teams, who want five racehorses out there to get quick outlet passes off opponents' missed shots, then hurry downcourt and shoot while they have a numbers advantage. Each coach has his own system, and many players in junior college don't exactly fit into any given system. In fact, many of them don't *want* to fit into a system but rather play a wide open, wild, playground style of ball. The truth be known, most players want to play this kind of ball, but the good ones realize that you have to have a system to win consistently. So, then, the challenge for a junior college coach like Jerry Stone was to pull these mavericks together, teach them some discipline, and do his best to harness all this wild energy into a cohesive team unit.

We got started right away. One big difference between major and junior college ball is that major schools can only practice from mid-October through the end of a season. Not so in junior college, where you can practice every single school day if you want. Stone took advantage of this, which was wise, because we had a lot to learn. Except for Lance and Puntus, our entire squad was freshmen, wide-eyed 18-year-olds who ran the gamut from cocky to scared stiff.

I felt lost. Stone was throwing all sorts of new plays and new techniques at us, and it was all foreign to me. We had never run a single play at Wilmer Hutchins; with all due respect to Coach Homer Smith, his technique consisted of throwing a ball out onto the court and saying, "Have at it, boys." Now all of a sudden, this white guy with long sideburns and western shirts is trying to teach me how to play basketball! Working on picks—how to set them, how to avoid them—learning defensive techniques against bigger players, honing your form on a jump shot; a million different aspects of the game I had never really practiced, but just performed (or tried to perform) by instinct. It was uncomfortable to be going through these exercises when I wasn't sure how to do something, and that was a very strange sensation for me; the basketball court had always been a place of complete comfort. Now I almost felt as if basketball were another subject for me, like history or economics.

But I listened closely to everything Stone said, because I wanted to learn. I had long ago dedicated myself totally to basketball, and if this man had knowledge that would improve my game, he had my complete attention.

The blackboard had "TEAM" written on it in large white letters, and Coach Stone was pounding his chalk under that word to make his point. Even though most of us had been the big stars of our high school teams, we were now members of a *unit*, a sacred collection of different elements known as a (pound chalk again) "Team!" None of us would be required to carry the scoring or rebounding burdens, as they would be shared. Like it or not, we would learn to play unselfish basketball.

I liked it. In high school, I had the responsibility to score, which can produce a sort of single-mindedness about the game. All you think of is, "How can I score this time?" Now I was learning new aspects of the game, opening up to include the special talents of my teammates. I realized I had a knack for seeing the whole court, anticipating where the next open spot might be and quickly passing to the player going to that spot. Over time, getting assists became just as important to me as getting points.

We were all developing, and there were so many of us! I remember Puntus wondering aloud to Coach Stone one day, "Hey, Coach, don't you think we've got a few too many players?" Stone laughed, but he knew two things: One, this team needed all the help it could get, and two, homesickness and other disenchantments of youth would deplete the ranks before long. He was right on both counts.

When the season started, we had 14 players, which was a good number. Who of the 14 would play was another question. Stone did decide that the little guy from Dallas would start the first game, and I applauded that decision. I also scored 21 points to lead the team, and we whipped McMurry JV, 99–80. We managed to win our next game, then went on a losing streak, dropping three straight. Coach Stone was substituting like crazy, trying to find the right combination of players among the "dirty dozen" wild freshmen he had. After last year's great season it must have looked like the talent had all graduated, and everyone seemed to think Midland was in for a mediocre year.

At the Amarillo Tournament our fortunes improved a bit; we won our first two games. In the finals, we met our nemesis, Amarillo College, which was nationally-ranked and undefeated. It was a tight game, but they took over in the fourth quarter and won by 6 points. We were now 5–3 going into our first conference game against the preseason favorite, South Plains.

A Wilmer Hutchins boy personally cleaned South Plains' clock, but it wasn't me, it was a guy about a foot taller: Chester Smith. After graduating from high school, Chester had determined that he had had enough education. For the next year he roamed around, doing some odd jobs and turning down various coaches who knew what kind of talent he had and tried to persuade him to try college. Chester, who is almost as bull-headed as I am, would have none of it. He was just a likable, lazy kid who was perfectly satisfied to hang out with his buddies, being playful and highsiding the day away. Fortunately for everyone concerned, Jerry Stone changed Chester's mind.

That night against South Plains, Chester had 20 points and 18 rebounds, a one-man wrecking crew who surprised his own teammates as much as he did our opponent. His physical skills were always there, but now it seemed his heart was catching up to make him complete. Among the team, there was talk of Chester being a pro prospect.

Next on the schedule was our own tournament, the Chaparral Classic. Barton College and Amarillo had both won their tournaments, and we thought it was only fair if we won ours. So we did, and three more wins were racked up before we faced Amarillo College again, this time on our home court. Amarillo was still undefeated and ranked first in our conference. They came into Chap Center on December 10 looking awesome, and they played great, but our fans kept us in the game. I told you those wildcatters could make some noise, and all 5,000 seats were filled for this one. Amarillo led through most of the game; we fought back and had a chance to win the game right before the buzzer, but the shot was wide and we went into over-time. Three players had fouled out, and we lost the game in OT, 91—86. One more win before the Christmas break put us at 10—5 on the season.

What did I do over Christmas vacation? I played bas-ketball every day. There was so much to work on, and I resolved not to spend all my holiday time wandering around a mall looking at things I couldn't afford.

Besides, who could think about shopping when there was basketball! Thoughts of the last four months filled my mind as I assessed my new position as a "college basket-ball player." First, I realized that I was better than I thought, proving something I *suspected* was true. "These guys put on their pants one leg at a time, just like I do," I considered. I knew that even though many of them had superior talent, I could beat them with quickness and in-telligence. I would work harder than they would, and my devotion would be my secret weapon.

I'm not sure I consciously resolved this, but during this time my heart and soul were completely given over to the game. The court became my home, and the benches and the baskets were more familiar than my sofa and televi-sion. In the gym I had a sense of belonging, and a deep knowledge that this is where my destiny would be fulfilled. Often after a long workout, I would linger around the gym, shooting free throws or jump shots and drinking in the essence of that place. When I was playing, I knew exactly what to do at every moment, and when I made a mistake, I knew exactly what had gone wrong; I loved the clarity in that.

Who could invent a more perfect game? In basketball, you are stripped of everything except pure athleticism; there are no clubs to swat with, no gloves to help you catch, and certainly no pads or helmets to protect you from the blows and scrapes you encounter. You are as nearly naked as you can be, and the crowd sees *everything*. The people in the stands are so close to the action that in any given game, you're bound to run into them and knock them over. They see your grief, your anger, your exaltation, your blood. And whatever you do, you hear their words—there are no dugouts to hide in, no crowd of players to be lost among. You are one row in front of the heckling, the name-calling, the cheers and adoration. In basketball you have only yourself to use, only your pure ability and desire with which to beat the man in front of you.

And yet you are on a team! With all the individual challenges, there is that extra dimension of the group, working together for a common goal. You need them, depend on them. So rather than the nerve-racking solitude of tennis or golf, you have partners in this enterprise of victory. Yes, there is loneliness, but when the buzzer sounds at the end of a game, you have a shoulder to lean on in defeat, and a comrade to hug in victory. I enjoy the sharing, the exchange of comments and criticisms among teammates after each contest. It helps you put things into perspective, and to learn a little more after each and every game.

Most of all, I love the way basketball offers you so many ways to excel: You can score points, make assists, grab rebounds, block shots, make steals, force turnovers, play good defense, set picks—so many ways to contribute, and so many ways to atone when one part of your game is not working. Looking back to my childhood—those days spent at the Turnkey Boys Club playing football, baseball, and even boxing—I can see that I was looking for something to excel in. Deep down inside I felt a yearning to be great somehow, in some sport. And here it was, the most unlikely sport of all! This game, which is predicated on height more than any other, was now fulfilling my dream to excel, and I delighted in it. All through my career, people would ask, "How do you do it? What enables you to compete in this sport at this level?" The answer is simple. I gave myself over to the game, and it gave itself back to me.

Hard work brings rewards, and after the Christmas break I was the leading scorer in three of our first four games. We won them all, and we did it with only nine players. During the break, seven players had either flunked out or dropped out, and so Coach Stone had a much easier time deciding who would play. "The only things which can keep you off the court," he announced, "are death, disease, and zebras [referees]. Hopefully, you can control at least two of those."

Foul trouble was becoming a problem, especially with yours truly. I could make the excuse that I was just "playing aggressively," but the truth is that smart players rarely foul out. No one does their team any good while sitting on the bench. So the message was sent out—especially to me and Puntus since we were the leading scorers—that we needed to stop fouling so much. But we weren't the only ones who had to watch the fouls; word filtered down from Amarillo that they had suffered mass departures as well, and now had only *six* players. They kept on winning but a showdown was inevitable.

We traveled to Amarillo to meet the Badgers on their home court, and the conference lead was on the line. Amarillo is up in the Texas Panhandle, which is deep-freeze area in early February. In junior college, you're not getting the Waldorf-Astoria and first-class airfare anyway, but our locker room was chilly by meat-locker standards. Our team space heater was Coach Stone, who had been psychologically preparing us for this game for two months. It was the big one we had to win if we were going to become a truly class team.

The first half started slowly, then broke wide open. Because of their limited number of players, Amarillo tried to slow things down so their players wouldn't run out of energy late in the game. We ran as much as possible, and at the beginning of the fourth quarter, the score was tied. Into the last few minutes, our two sophomores led the way, as Puntus poured in 27 points and Lance snagged 10 rebounds. Still neither team could get any kind of big lead. Coach Stone was worried that we lacked the killer instinct, saying that we needed to "put teams away" when we had the chance. We never got that with Amarillo, though, and with just 10 seconds left, the score was tied, 86–86. Puntus inbounded the ball to me, and I headed upcourt. Eight seconds. I looked for an open man, but everyone was covered. Now at the top of the key, I saw a small opening up the middle and decided to take it inside. Four seconds left. I sliced through two men and took off for the bucket and bam! One of the Amarillo post men made a clumsy attempt to block my shot and fouled me "with feeling." Two seconds left, and the conference title is on the line. I'm at the free throw with two chances, and 6,000 insane people are screaming bloody murder for me to MISS IT! MISS IT!

All I could think was, "I love moments like this." Two teams play an entire game—heck, an entire *season*—and it comes down to me shooting a couple of free throws. Standing at the line I felt all the tension, all that anticipation of these shots—and I felt powerful, because I knew I would make them. At times like these, when more emotional people get wobbly, my natural calm comes to the rescue. I sank both shots and Amarillo couldn't get a shot off before the buzzer sounded. The Good Guys win again.

Exactly one week later, we won two games in one night. Huh? Well it went like this: We had made the long trek up to that famous resort town, Borger, Texas, and beaten Frank Phillips College, 90–81, and on the way home we learned that Independence College, who had beaten us in our third game of the season, had used an ineligible player, and therefore had to forfeit the win. We all jumped up and down and congratulated each other as if we had just beaten Notre Dame. We were winning, and everything was going our way.

The ragtag group now found itself in the Region V Tournament. We had a 27–4 record, and we were playing like we knew what we were doing. In fact, maybe a bit of cockiness was creeping in.

This wasn't a good sign, and to make matters worse, our first opponent was Clarendon, a "sleeper" team that we had beaten twice during the regular season. Like a poor relative or an old girlfriend, a team like this can come out of nowhere and start causing trouble in a hurry. We didn't take these guys too seriously, and sure enough, Clarendon had us down by 11 points at halftime. Coach Stone came into the locker room mad as hell, and he broke a box or two of chalk as he pounded on the blackboard, diagramming plays and saying "I told you! I told you!" repeatedly. We got humble real fast.

Clarendon was doing everything possible to slow the game down, and with 15 minutes to play they had us down by 15 points. Then we shifted from second gear directly into fifth, and the race was on. I led the way with 18 points, and a pretty vicious dunk that got everybody going. But it was my roomie, Rodney McChriston, who really deserves the credit. Rodney was a quiet, determined young guy from Memphis, Tennessee, who was pretty depressed because he hadn't gotten to play much all season. Now suddenly we're in the play-offs and we're losing, and the coach sends in Rodney, off the bench cold, and tells him to make something happen. That's a huge order, but Rodney hustled in and promptly hit four straight jumpers, and the bench couldn't believe it. You mean this guy has been sitting down all year? C'mon! Anyway, the booster rockets had fired and we left Clarendon wondering what had happened, 72–63.

In the second round, we cruised past Frank Phillips College (Now wait a minute: Who would come up with a name for a school like that? Do you think Frank did?), beating them 77–65. Chester, who was playing every minute of every game, was awesome, scoring 27 points with 21 rebounds. The folks back in The Hutch would have been proud.

The next game was the regional championship, the last step before the national tournament. Our foe was Cisco College, a team that had rapidly improved toward the end of the year. A bigger factor was the media and fan pressure, because Midland had been in the regional championship game three times in the last five years and never brought home the title. I have to credit Coach Stone, though; if he was nervous, he never showed it.

Cisco was a running team and the pace of the game was fast and furious. Neck-and-neck most of the way, it was a demanding game for all of us, and I played with total, reckless abandon. If a ball was on the floor, I leaped for it; I was lunging for steals, for blocked shots, and I made a few driving jump shots that even I couldn't believe went in. It was down to the wire again, and we had an 83–81 lead with just a few seconds remaining when Cisco sent up the tying shot—and missed. We had dodged a bullet, and Midland had its first regional championship. It was a sweet moment made even better by the fact I was named Most Valuable Player of the tournament and Chester, Puntus, and I all made the All-Tournament team. We had awards, we had a title, we had confidence, and we had plane tickets to Hutchinson, Kansas, for the NJCAA national tournament.

Unlike the NCAA Final Four championship, which moves to a different site each year, the NJCAA tournament has found a home in Hutchinson, Kansas, and these people take it *seriously*. For one week every year, the town shuts down and goes basketball bonkers. The players, trainers, and coaches are treated like visiting royalty, and you can't walk 10 feet anywhere without someone asking for an autograph or offering to buy you lunch or dinner. The top 16 teams in the country are there, and like the hosts, the competitors are at fever pitch.

When UCLA or Notre Dame goes to the Final Four, they usually fly first class. We flew coach, but it hardly mattered to us. We were so excited we could hardly stand it. We pulled up to our hotel, the Holiday Inn, and the airport bus fell silent as we got our first glimpse of Yvon Joseph, the 6'10" All-American center for the nation's top-ranked team, Miami-Dade College. He was huge, bigger than any player we had faced all year, and it suddenly hit us: How in the world are we going to compete against talent like that?

Coach Stone saw us whispering about Joseph, and he got mad. He stormed to the back of the bus, and ordered everybody out into the parking lot.

"All right, we're here. Yes, that's Yvon Joseph, he's huge, and he's probably the best player in this tournament. But let me tell you guys something. *You're the best team.* You've proved it all year, and now you're going to prove it to everybody here. Stop admiring other players and look at yourselves—you're the best!"

Then he turned to me. "Spud, I promise you, when this

week is over, everyone's gonna know about you. You're the quickest player I've ever seen, and no one can guard you. That's it."

We stood there for a moment, not moving. Stone was intense, we had never seen him this way before. No question he was a winner (his record at Midland was 276–67, a phenomenal .805 winning percentage), but here he was, in all earnestness, telling us *we were the best team.* We felt those words in our bones. Our team was definitely the underdog of the tournament, having only nine players and having won so many big games by hairbreadth margins. Furthermore, Chester was our tallest player, and at 6'6" he was constantly guarding guys much taller and heavier than he was, a chore I could relate to. To make things even tougher, our first game was against the defending national champions, the Westark Roadrunners from Fort Smith, Arkansas. Anchoring their team was DeWayne Shepard, last year's MVP in the national tournament. We gave him to Chester.

It was a game I will never forget, because it had such wild tides of momentum and plenty of strange occurences. Early in the game we took our time, playing a more patient style and hitting 65 percent of our shots. As usual Puntus led the way, hitting from every spot on the floor, and suddenly we had a 13-point lead. Westark, 32–4 on the season, pulled within 10 at the half.

The mood in the locker room was electric. We were beating the national champs and all cylinders were running smooth. Chester had held Shepard in check and when the buzzer sounded for the second half to begin, we went out on the floor ready to run. And run we did. Jerome Crowe, the fifth starter with Chester, Lance, Puntus, and me, hit two big shots and I added some more to give us a whopping 21-point margin with only about 10 minutes to go. Then, just as quickly as we had built up our lead, it disappeared.

Basketball is a game of streaks, and it takes a long time to get used to that. Some fans never do, and they have heart attacks when they see a big lead blown. I'm sure many Midland fans thought the end was near when Westark started hitting every shot they threw up, eight in a row, to pull within five. I wasn't much help at this point: I missed 8, count 'em, 8 out of 15 free throws. I usually shoot pretty well from the line, about 75 percent, so I cringed at the thought of tomorrow's headline, "Webb Strangles Himself, Team, with Bush League Choke Performance at Free-Throw Line." But as I said, in basketball there are many ways to excel, so I quickly found something other than free throws. Like an alley-oop pass to Puntus for a dunk, then a breakaway slam dunk of my own, then a short jumper followed by—what d'ya know? —two made free throws.

But for every basket I made, Westark answered with one of their own. With 40 seconds left, it was 71–68 and I managed to miss two more free throws (just to keep it close, you understand—it's more exciting that way) and Westark's Tony Kelleybrew hit a jumper to make it a 1-point game with 24 seconds left. On the next possession, Puntus was fouled, and he missed the first free throw. Then came the play of plays, more dramatic than a season-ending episode of *Dallas*.

Puntus offers up his second free throw, which bounces wildly off the rim into the hands of a Westark player. He takes two dribbles downcourt, and as I step in front of him he passes the ball off to Kelleybrew, then promptly runs me over like a lumber truck. As I go splattering to the floor, I see Kelleybrew streaking upcourt, with Puntus giving chase, trying to swat the ball from behind.

Then, from the left side of the basket, Kelleybrew reaches up to lay in an uncontested lay-up. As the ball leaves his hand, everyone in the place knows we've lost. That is, everyone but Puntus, who comes out of nowhere, stretching every last inch of himself until his whole upper body is *above the rim,* and blocks Kelleybrew's shot against the glass. As both players descend to earth, for one split second every eye in the arena is on the official under the basket. The buzzer sounds, and no goal-tending call is made—we've won! Our bench empties, the stands empty, and it's total bedlam. We're crying and hugging each other, people we don't even know are picking us up and cheering, and the Westark team is watching it all, stunned. They had managed to overcome a 21-point lead, but just fell one point shy. The Chaps? We became the Cinderella team of the tournament, and the good people of Hutchinson adopted us as their own team. From that moment on, it was as if we had home court advantage the rest of the way.

You cannot witness a miracle and not feel charmed by it. Puntus' amazing block had all of us bound in a sort of euphoric state, and we shared a sense that anything to come would be anticlimactic. However, there was another game to play, this one against Dixie College, which isn't in Alabama or Georgia—it's in Utah. These guys were all white, so we figured we had to show them some soul.

We led the whole way, and even though Dixie came back to tie it twice, we never lost control. We also hit 21 of 26 free throws, so we had learned our lesson from the game before. As for the soul, Puntus and I traded dunks with each other, while Chester had a career-high 28 points and pulled down 17 rebounds. In the newspaper article the next day, Chester was quoted as saying, "They thought I could whip my man, and I'm glad I could do the job." Short and sweet, vintage Chester.

I woke the morning after the Dixie game, and someone had put a copy of the *Hutchinson News* outside my door. I opened it up to find a big story entitled "Spud-itis: Everyone's Catching It." Media attention was still something new to me, and I got a kick out of how they made such a big deal about everything. Still, this was an article not about our team, but about me, and I realized that people really were amazed by what I was doing. Already that season I had blocked 20 shots and recorded over 40 dunks, and yet people were quoted as saying they "didn't believe a person his size could dunk a basketball." Well, heck, what had I been doing all season? I enjoyed the attention, but it also confused me. In my mind, I was just going about my business, playing the game the only way I know how to play.

That wasn't the only news I got that morning. Coach Stone came and told us that Lance had just been to the doctor, and he had fractured a bone in his neck and could not play the rest of the tournament. That was quite a blow, because Lance had provided strong leadership all year long. He was bright and expressed himself well; he was a true motivator who knew how to get a team fired up. Hearing the news, Puntus and I looked at each other with expressions that said, "Uh-oh," because we knew this meant neither of us would get even a minute's rest in the next two games. Oh, well. . . .

In the semifinal game we were facing a big, strong team from Indiana—Vincennes College. Everyone knows what a basketball-crazy state Indiana is, and this school had that same long-standing tradition of hoops excellence. They were resourceful, just the kind of team that might jump up and surprise you, and before the game I could tell that Coach Stone was a little nervous. Lance was out, and we were so close to that title game you could just taste it.

Vincennes had a 6'8" post man named Courtney Witte, and he was going to give Chester all he could handle. The rest of us were just hanging on, hoping we had the stamina to go the distance with these Midwesterners. For the first 7 minutes we stayed close, but never ahead. Then, with 12 minutes left in the half, we caught fire and went on a 20–2 scoring spree that put us up at halftime, 40–30. In the second half, we came out playing okay, but somewhere we hit a time warp: The team was playing in slow motion and the hard-charging guys from Vincennes ran right past us. For 9 minutes we couldn't hit a thing, and the Trail-blazers took the lead, 58–55. We needed something dramatic to happen.

Ask and ye shall receive.

Mr. Chester "Cheddar Cheese" Smith hit a jumper, was fouled, and nailed the free throw to tie the score. Then another jumper from Puntus from 18 feet. Swish. And to top it off, a swooping steal from the leading carrier of Spud-itis, which I took the length of the floor and jammed as hard as I could. The crowd went wild, and the underdogs from Midland were on their way to the championship game.

"Saturday night's all right for fightin', get a little action in . . ."

Music from the radio filtered through a small jam box sitting by a stack of towels in the locker room. There were lockers for 16 players, but tonight only 8 were filled, and the players sitting in front of the lockers were quiet. The clock said 7:28 P.M., and in 47 minutes the 8 members of the Midland Chaparral basketball team would begin playing for the national championship.

Our opponent was Miami-Dade College of Miami, Florida, the undefeated number-one ranked team in the country. Miami had a full lineup of great players, led by the towering All-American post man, 6'10" Yvon Joseph. He would be guarded by our tallest man, the "Cheddar," who had played virtually every single minute of the last 20 games.

The scoring punch was to come from three men whose average weight was 156 pounds, dripping wet. Two of those players had been in every single game from start to finish, the other had played only 30 minutes of basketball in the last three months. The line on the game was Miami-Dade by seven points.

Hutchinson Arena was sold out with the biggest crowd in its history, 7,800. The arena only holds 7,500, but the demand for tickets was so high that 300 extra standing-room-only tickets were made available to a hoops-hungry Kansas town. The national media was there, coaches from several major colleges were there, and most importantly, three members of my family were there: Stephanie, Renee, and Bean. Once again, when I needed it, my family support was there.

Just before tip-off, I looked around the bench and couldn't believe how "underdog" we looked. Our scrawny, road-weary starters; our three reserves who, loyal as hound dogs, had warmed the bench all year with little or no playing time; our leader, Lance, sitting in street clothes with a huge neck brace on; and Jerry Stone, our coach, who had almost lost his voice, and who had just gotten his assistant coach three days earlier after coaching the whole year by himself. I almost felt sorry for us myself.

Except I knew what we had inside. We knew we were good, and we had that key ingredient: We believed we could win. That had been Stone's gift to us in the locker room. No big speeches, no special strategy; he told us from his gut that he believed in our ability, and with all his experience in basketball, he looked at us and saw winners. As for me, I had prayed before the game and I felt that God had set my path to this point. I felt very positive, and in control of what was about to happen. Just before tip-off, I told myself that I was already a champion; now it was time to prove that to this crowd and to the world.

From the first minute, the noise in the arena was the loudest I'd ever heard. Then on their first possession, mountain man Yvon Joseph goes up for a jump shot, and Jerome Crowe blocks it! Even more noise. We get the loose ball, dribble up court, and the pass goes to Rodney McChriston, who buries a jumper—swish! Rodney was filling in for Lance and doing a super job. The underdogs were here to play, and the crowd was shaking the gym foundation with their cheering.

The pregame jitters were gone and it was down to business. We controlled the game most of the first half, building up an eight point lead, but Miami shaved it down to four at the half, 47–43. As we made our way to the locker room for halftime, people were yelling at us, "You can do it!" and "We love you, Midland!" I glanced over at Puntus and his expression said, "Can you believe all this?" No one in that gym could believe we were winning, and we couldn't believe the crowd was being so wonderfully hysterical about it.

Some of us sat in the locker room, other players were lying down. Coach Stone looked us in the eye and calmly said, "Okay, we're going to win. Now, here is how we're going to control the second half . . . " We all listened without saying a thing. When Stone finished, several players walked by where Lance was sitting and said, "We're going to whip these guys for you, man. We're gonna get you a victory." Lance looked up at them, tilting his aching neck back as far as he could. "Don't just talk about it, you guys," he said. "I can't use talk. Go out there and *do it*!" With that we piled out of the locker room, ready for the most important half of basketball any of us had ever played.

We started the second half by holding the ball, using a play pattern from an old Boston Celtics game in the 1950s. Red Auerbach was coaching, and the only player he trusted to handle the ball was Bob Cousy, and so a post man came out to the free-throw line and passed the ball back and forth to Cousy, who dribbled the time away on the clock. Miami was in a 1-3-1 zone defense and our makeshift offensive plan worked to perfection. Chester would come out and pass me the ball; I would dribble all over the place until I spotted an opening in the zone. Then I zipped the pass to whoever was open for the easy shot. Not only did this offense work time off the clock, it gave the other four players time to rest while I dribbled around and Miami defenders chased me.

After a while they began to get frustrated, and I was getting fouled like crazy. In all, I made 18 trips to the foul line, and hit 16 of them. Coming down the stretch, you've got to make those foul shots.

It was a thrilling second half, with both teams giving every last ounce of effort. We managed to hold on to a slim lead, but the Falcon players kept shaving it back down with some remarkable plays. With only 4:43 remaining in the game, Miami had pulled to within one point, making the score 71–70. A minute later, I almost got killed.

We had called a time-out, and both coaches were trying to settle their teams down for the homestretch. My teammates and I were tired, at least our bodies were tired. But our minds were *focused,* and no one was hanging his head or loafing over to the sideline the way you do when you're really beat. We were alert, and anxious to see how the next four minutes would unfold.

After the time-out, Miami got the ball and drove in for a lay-up, which they missed. I was under the basket, and I was leaping high for the rebound, when *wham!* I got hammered by a Miami forward who I guess was sick and tired of the way I'd jumped over him all night so he had decided to keep me near the ground where he thought I belonged. Well, it worked. I went down in a heap and the referees called a foul and ran over to see if I was okay.

I was more than okay, I was mad. So were my teammates, and a fight nearly broke out. Now, I'm not one to back away from a fight, even though most people would say that is the intelligent thing to do if you are 5′4″ and 120 pounds, but I was flat on my back and that's not too safe when a bunch of angry basketball giants start stomping their big feet around. I rolled off the court and picked myself up as the crowd showered boos upon the Miami big man who flattened the little guy. My revenge came once again at the free throw line, where I hit both ends of a 1-and-1 to put us up, 73–70.

A minute later, Miami had scored twice and went on top with their first lead of the ballgame, 74–73. The Miami fans went wild, screaming their approval with deafening howls. "We've got to take it to 'em," I thought to myself, and I pushed the ball upcourt as fast as I could, taking it straight to the hole. Once again I got clobbered, but made both my foul shots to put us back ahead by one.

An acrobatic steal by Puntus followed by a soaring lay-up gave us a three-point lead with only 24 seconds left. Miami-Dade brought the ball down, shot, and missed. There was a mad scramble for the loose ball, and it ended in a jump ball. All eyes turned toward the scorer's table, where the red arrow signaling possession (according to the alternate possession rule) was pointing . . . in our direction! Only 17 seconds left, and the game was ours!

With a three-point lead, all we had to do was hold the ball and run out the clock. The last thing you want, with 7,800 fans screaming their lungs out, with the national championship just 17 ticks away, is for some guy to have his brain short-circuit and detach from his body just long enough for that body to take a totally unnecessary, crazy fool shot. Unfortunately, that is exactly what I did.

I don't know what got into me, except the shot was there and it felt right and I took it. And of course it missed. And of course Miami got the rebound. And of course they took the ball down and mountain man Yvon Joseph scored while Puntus was hanging all over him, giving him a chance for a three-point play. And of course he made the free throw and the game was tied with three seconds left. We had a chance to win it, but turned over the ball.

So all of a sudden we aren't national champs, we're national chumps. For 47 minutes and 47 seconds we played brilliant ball, and now here we are facing overtime against a well-rested team with twice as many healthy players. Coach Stone had to be thinking, "How could you guys possibly blow this one?" But he never said a word. In the huddle, he mapped out our strategy, and reminded Puntus and me that we were both in foul trouble with four fouls, and if we fouled out it would be doomsday. The buzzer sounded, and we charged back in to get the job done.

Chester hit the first bucket of the overtime, then Miami came back with a bucket by their hot-shooting guard, Emery Atkinson. With only 48 seconds left, Miami stole the ball and scored again on a lay-up, and we were facing another last-shot situation. Twenty seconds left, and the crowd is pounding the gym seats into submission and yelling like rodeo cowboys. I passed off, then got the ball back. Fourteen seconds. I locked in on the basket, and just as 6′10″ Yvon Joseph came flying out at me, I released a 25-foot levitation jumper that arced high over Joseph's flailing arms. The shot dropped right in the center of the net, and once again it was tied. We were going to a *second* overtime.

By now the Hutchinson Sports Arena was crazy, simply beserk. No one expected us to even be in the game, and yet we were giving Miami-Dade the fight of their lives. It was just too much.

Midland got the ball first, and without even thinking about it I raced downcourt and planted a 15-foot jumper. Jerome Crowe added a free throw, and we were up by three. It didn't last long, as Atkinson hit an inside shot for the Falcons, bringing the margin to one point. On the next play, doomsday arrived—Puntus fouled out.

Off the bench came Justin Morett, a 6′5″ freshman who was the only Midland native on the team, having led his Midland High team to a championship his senior year. But now the stakes were much higher, and with a team leader like Puntus out of the lineup, a lot of fans thought the show was over.

I knew I had to take over the game. Coach Stone looked at me and nodded, as if to say, "I know what you're thinking, and you're right." The Miami-Dade bench was hollering, pointing out at skinny, pale Justin Morett and saying they were going to eat him alive. The referee blew the whistle, and with 2:38 left on the game clock I went charging downcourt.

Somewhere just past the free-throw line, I took off as the Miami defense closed in around me. I saw the shot kiss the backboard and drop, and as I landed I never slowed down even a step, but raced back up the sidelines, heading off the Miami offense and stepping in front of a pass. The steal was just what we needed, and as I jammed the ball through the hoop, everyone wearing Midland College green and gold leaped into the air, roaring their delight. We were up by five.

Just under two minutes remained, and Atkinson hit still another inside shot to trim the lead back to three. Miami added a free throw and suddenly the score was 88–86. Now it was time for another of our ragtag team members to rise to the occasion; this time, the unlikely hero was Midland's native son, Justin Morett.

Fighting his way to the bucket, Morett was hacked by a Miami player and sent to the line. Talk about your pressure situations. Reserve player. Freshman. Deafening noise. Only 32 seconds left, and the national championship hanging in the balance. The first shot bounced off the rim, but while the Miami fans jeered, Justin buried the second to give us a critical three-point edge. It was real courage on his part.

Now only 24 seconds remained, and Atkinson had the ball and a determined look in his eye. He went up for the shot and I swatted it off course, but fouled him in the process. Five fouls, and I was out of the game.

That might have been a moment of dejection for me, but instead the crowd made it one of my greatest triumphs. The entire arena, fans and foes alike, rose to their feet and gave me a standing ovation I shall never forget. The game stopped, and all eyes watched as I left the court and plopped down on the bench. I had played this game with every ounce of energy in my body and I think these people knew it. As I sat there, feeling the backslaps of my teammates and the love of those Kansas basketball fans, I never felt taller in my life.

As if to make my moment complete, Atkinson missed the free throw and Chester, the old reliable, grabbed the rebound and was fouled. He hit both free throws like the coolest cat in the alley and we had the lead and the game. John Jones of the Falcons got a lay-up with four seconds left, but Chester had drawn another foul and he sank both freebies to make the final score Midland, 93, Miami-Dade, 88.

We were national champions!

Two things stand out in my mind about the end of the game. The first was when Puntus fouled out, and came over to sit next to Coach Stone. Those two had been through a lot over the past couple of years, and they had a very strong bond of friendship. This would be their last game together, and as Puntus sat down, Coach Stone looked him right in the eye and said, "As soon as this game is over, I'm gonna come over and give you a hug so hard your back will break." Puntus smiled his wide, happy smile. When the game ended, Stone and his prized sophomore bear-hugged like a father and son.

The other story is about Chester, who always had his own way of doing things. After he was fouled with just four seconds left, Stone called the team over to strategize the last play, as anything can happen in basketball. He looked around for Chester, only to spot him at the end of the bench, digging through the trainer's bag. The buzzer sounded and as Chester galloped in to shoot his free throws, we all could see the pair of scissors tucked in his sock. Make no mistake, when the final second ticked away, "Cheddar" headed straight for the basket, scissors in hand, to cut down the net. It would be his personal trophy.

There were plenty of awards left to give. After receiving the gigantic trophy as national champions, the tournament officials named Puntus as the Most Valuable Player of the tourney and Coach Stone as Coach of the Tournament. Both Puntus and I made the All-Tournament team, and I was named the Outstanding Small Player, which is given to the player "displaying good character, leadership, and loyalty to his fellow players and coaches." The player also has to be 6'1" or shorter, which means I had room to grow.

Looking back at the pictures of our team taken just after the game, you can see how exhausted we all were. Everyone, except for the coaches, is lying down on the floor, slumped like bums in an alley. We had played four games in five days with only eight players, and each of the games was a hard-fought, down-to-the-wire contest. When the photographer said "Smile," I saw someone roll over and say, "I'm too tired to smile." He wasn't kidding.

Next to winning a championship, bringing home the trophy to your fans is the greatest feeling of all. It's different for each person, but for me it took a couple of days to realize what the team had accomplished, and what I had done as a freshman player. In the Midland airport when we arrived, the crowd was going nuts, hugging and kissing all the players, and reporters were scrambling to ask the standard, obvious question, "Hey, how does it feel?" And only because you really do feel so wonderful, you can't be sarcastic and say, "Awful. I'm deeply disappointed that we just won the national championship." Instead you grin your fool head off and yell, "Great, man, it feels great!"

One TV reporter did stick a microphone in my face and say, "Spud, what business do you have being on the court with these players?" I guess he was trying to have fun, but I responded, "I was wondering what business they have being out there with *me*." That sounds pretty cocky, but that's how I felt. Winning a national is so much work, with so much sacrifice involved, your feelings aren't just some warm glowing sense of "Isn't that nice. We're number one." You think back to all the practices, the running, the drills, the road trips in creaky buses, the nail-biting finishes to half a dozen different games and to all the times you were tired or beaten down and then found that extra ounce of energy to get back on the floor and give it everything you had.

Because that's what it takes to win a championship—everything. If you aren't totally dedicated to that goal, and willing to pay the price for it, you won't win. And of course, it takes a little luck. That becomes part of the good feeling, too—that for one season, at least, the breaks went your way.

So what did I feel once it all soaked in? First, that all the hard work was worth it. That gives an athlete a sense of completeness, the feeling that you got back everything you put into the season, and more. Second, I felt we deserved it. We had every disadvantage and we still came out on top. Finally, I was proud of myself. Less than two years ago, I had been told I was too small to play even high school basketball. Now, I was a team leader for the NJCAA National Champions.

When everybody your whole life tells you something, like "you're too small" or "you're too clumsy," it's hard not to start believing that yourself. Deep in my heart I always knew I could be great, and finally I had proved it. From that moment on, I resolved I would never listen to another critic again. Whatever I could dream, I could achieve.

8

Everything Falls Apart

I never intended to stay at Midland more than a year, but after winning the national championship, there were suddenly lots of reasons to stay. Secretly, though, I had hoped that a major college would have noticed my accomplishments as a freshman and offered me a scholarship. No such luck. Maybe they thought I was too tall or something.

I had come home to Dallas some sort of hero, which was fun. Everyone in the neighborhood was stopping by the house, saying how proud they were, and around the Soul Mart all the customers were telling Dad what a great kid he had. The one place where nothing changed—where nothing ever changes, no matter how famous you get—is the Highland Hills gym. That's what I love about that place: No matter how big-time you become, you still have to prove yourself every time you set foot on the floor. Nobody gives you anything.

As always, my main playing partner was Mookie, and he was trying to convince me to transfer to North Texas State University, where he was set to start at shooting guard. Since our earliest days of playing together, we had dreamed of being on the same college team, zipping passes back and forth, making up our own plays. What's more, I was close to the NTSU coach, Bill Blakeley, who had repeatedly told me that he thought I could be a standout in Division I ball. It was nice to have someone believe in me.

But there were obligations back in Midland. I had become very close to Coach Stone, not to mention my teammates and several of the Midland alumni. One couple in particular was John and Carolyn Hendricks.

There were a lot of wealthy oil families in Midland during those years, but not many were willing to let a black teenager come into their home and become part of the family. John and Carolyn did. I got to know them during my freshman year, and they listened one night as I told them how close I was to my family back in Dallas and how homesick I was. Even though our backgrounds were as different as day and night, the Hendricks and I shared our strong Christian faith; they kind of adopted me over the year, and I spent a lot of time at their home. They even gave me a key, and sometimes when I wanted to get away from campus, I would drive out to their huge house and raid the icebox and watch TV.

The Hendrickses had flown up to see me play in the national tourney in Kansas, and one real special moment for me was when Coach Stone passed along something Carolyn Hendricks had said. She'd told him, "Spud is a gift to me. I know God sent him to me and he has enriched and inspired us more than he'll ever know." Those words stayed with me, and the thought of leaving my second family really saddened me.

Pressure was building in that summer of 1982: Lots of people were telling me what I should do, and I couldn't make up my mind. Did I owe it to Midland to return? Would I be disloyal to leave? But what about my career: Wouldn't it be better served at a major college, and one closer to home? I was struggling hard with these emotions when Coach Stone called on the phone one day.

"Spud, how are you doing?"

I paused. "Not too good, coach. I'm confused."

"Do you want me to come over, Spud?" he asked, not wanting to pressure me.

"I wish you would," I said.

He was over in a flash.

We didn't talk very long, but just his being there made me feel better. Neither of us had to say much. I knew he wanted me back, but Stone is an unselfish coach who puts his players first, and he wouldn't stand in the way of a good offer from a major college.

In the end, I decided to return to Midland College. The people there had been so nice to me, and I believed there was still more I could learn from a good coach like Jerry Stone. Anyway, at the end of my sophomore year, I would be eligible to go to any major college in the country. My parents had mixed emotions. On the one hand, they liked NTSU because it would keep me close to Dallas. On the other hand, they weren't too sorry to see me get away from Mookie, who was quite a party man. My mother has always been the overprotective type, and she thought Mook was a bad influence on me; in Midland, all I had time for was books and basketball.

Well, I did find time for one other thing. Over the summer, on the Fourth of July to be exact, I had my first official date with a beautiful girl from Kimball High School named Dawn Baker. I had known about her through my buddy Charles, who had tried unsuccessfully to woo her for a couple of months before meeting another girl. Dawn and I had a lot of fun together, and I felt comfortable with her from the start. She used to kid me: "Hey, Spud, I thought everyone said you were shy. You sure don't act shy around me!"

Dawn and I wrote constantly once I went back to West Texas, and I would learn to appreciate her friendship more and more over the coming months. Very soon after the school year started, almost everything in my life began to fall apart.

September in Midland is only a little better than August, when temperatures climb to more than 100° and stubbornly stay there. The campus seemed somehow more barren than before; but my first week of classes was behind me, and on this Friday afternoon I was heading off to my dorm in search of shade and a cold drink. When I walked in the room, the phone was ringing. It was my sister, Janice.

"Spud, honey, something terrible has happened," she cried into the phone. "It's Dad. He's been arrested."

Now Janice, the oldest, doesn't usually lose control, but she was sobbing like crazy, saying something about drugs.

"What do you mean, he was selling drugs?" I yelled in disbelief. My father, the minister's son and biggest drug-hater of all time, had been arrested for pushing pills? I couldn't believe it.

The news was true, and the situation was bad. It seems that the Soul Mart had not been doing well, and Dad owed the Internal Revenue Service some back taxes. He was looking for new ways to improve business when a seedy character from the run-down neighborhood near the store came in and asked Dad if he wanted to sell some "diet pills" in his store.

The man, who was known around the area as being pretty sleazy, had quite a supply of these pills, which were actually prescription-only amphetamines; he probably had drug enforcement officials on his back and wanted to get rid of the stuff quick. He told Dad the pills were perfectly legal, and to sell them for $10 a bottle. Now my Dad's no fool, but he is very naive when it comes to drugs, and so he bought the whole load from the man and stocked them behind the counter.

The pills proved to be pretty popular, and soon the drug enforcement men were onto the fact that illegal pills were being sold out of the Soul Mart. One afternoon, the police sent an undercover cop in to get some pills, and Dad happily sold them to the man. Minutes later, Dad was being handcuffed and dragged down to jail.

No one was ever able to find the low-life guy who sold Dad the pills, and Dad ended up plea-bargaining his sentence after entering a guilty plea. Some of the cops who worked in the area knew Dad and said they thought he was probably ignorant of the fact that the pills were illegal, but it was a federal case and the FBI investigators maintained that Dad should have known better and checked the pills out more thoroughly before buying them and putting them out for sale.

That October day when Dad stood before the judge for sentencing was a bleak day for the Webb family. We all were crying as Dad stood there, so alone and so worried as the judge delivered a speech.

"Mr. Webb, I understand that you are a hard-working man trying to run your own business," said the judge. "But you ought to be ashamed of yourself, selling illegal narcotics without bothering to check them out."

The judge looked at all of us standing there and continued, "You obviously have a fine family. You've supported them, putting four children through college and providing a more than decent standard of living. So how does a good man like you get involved with drugs?"

We all wondered the same thing. It was just inconceivable that a man like Dad would be standing here in a courtroom facing *this* kind of charge—of all things!

Dad was given a two-year sentence, and sent to the

minimum security federal prison at Big Spring, Texas. He hung his head and apologized to the court, but it was really for us. Dad had worked so hard all his life but now here he was on his way to prison, and we all felt his shame. He was a proud man, and especially proud of the clean reputation he and his family had; to be the one in trouble with the law was more than he could bear.

The judge banged his gavel and another flood of tears let loose. We were all angry for what had happened, at the seeming injustice of it, and we were afraid for what might happen to Dad in prison. At least he was being sent to a prison for white-collar criminals, hardly a dangerous place at all. Most of the people there had been involved in some sort of business swindle or stock fraud, or were first-time offenders like Dad who were largely innocent though technically guilty. The place was known as "Club Fed" by other prisoners in the tougher Texas prisons, because it had nice, private rooms with televisions, a rec hall, very lenient rules regarding activities, and very few guards.

Still, it was a prison, and even with time off for good behavior Dad would be gone eight months. That meant all the kids would have to pitch in and help run the store. For Janice and Renee, it meant working two jobs, and Mom had to do extra work with her cleaning job to make ends meet. It wouldn't be easy.

Because of my college commitments—I had to play basketball or I would lose my scholarship—I felt really guilty that I could not be at home, helping to run the store. Once again, Mom would have to hold everything together with love and encouragement the way she always had. She told me not to worry, and Janice added some words of reassurance, so I went back to playing basketball. I was able to do one thing, however, and that was visit Dad, because Big Spring was only a 45-minute drive from Midland. I went up there four times during the seven and a half months Dad served, and we had some good talks in the visiting room of the prison.

What do you talk about in prison? Well, we talked a lot about my basketball, and where it was taking me. Dad had a good idea of what was going on because he watched all the games on the TV in the Big Spring rec hall, shouting at the set and telling all the other men about his son, the tiny star of the national champion Midland Chaparrals. They got a kick out of watching the games, which amused me: I never thought I'd be big in prisons.

Dad also got to know some of Texas' more notorious crooks, like Billie Sol Estes, the friend of Lyndon Johnson's who'd been nailed for mail fraud. There were also several men in for securities fraud, and Dad learned a lot about the stock market from them.

Soon after the trial I got a call from Mookie, who said he was going to be in Dallas and would go by and check on my family. He was going to help his mom with some things around the house while he had a day off from playing ball. He sounded up, and cocky as always. The phone rang the next day; it was Mookie again, but the voice was totally different.

It was shaking with emotion. Mookie's mom had just been killed.

He had waved good-bye to her as she drove off in the car to pick up something at the grocery. Two blocks from home, she had a heart attack and crashed into a light pole. Mookie, whose father had died when he was in seventh grade, was now without both parents.

Mookie was devastated, but there was more tragedy to come. Two weeks after his mother's funeral, his sisters were having an argument when one sister pulled out a gun. The yelling continued, and a shot was fired. Mookie's youngest sister went down, and had to be rushed to the hospital. She lived, but the feud between the sisters continued. Mookie told me he couldn't believe they were acting like that so soon after their mom had been killed.

Basketball might have been Mookie's salvation, but less than a week after the shooting, that, too, was taken away from him. During a practice, Mookie was scrimmaging against one of his teammates, and he went up to dunk. His teammate grabbed his left leg as he went up, and when Mookie landed his knee twisted in a grotesque way, tearing several muscles.

Mookie said later that it felt like he had "stepped in a hole, jammed for a moment, and then went all rubbery." The doctor told him it was a freak accident, a one-in-a-million injury that would be very tough to operate on. When he finally did undergo surgery, the doctors found that large knots had formed, and they had to cut away key muscle tissue during three hours of arthroscopic surgery. Because it was his left knee, his leaping knee, Mookie was told he would never be the same player again.

In less than three weeks, Mookie had seen his mother killed, his sister shot, and his basketball career ended. It scared me to see how quickly—how easily, how unpredictably—you could lose everything that was important to you. But now was not the time to think about myself.

Mookie had always looked after me, and it was time to return the favor. I called Mom, and asked her if Mookie could move in with us until his leg healed and he could get hold of himself. She said yes, and over the coming months our basketball friendship would become something much deeper. From our earliest days in The Projects of West Dallas, Mookie had always been someone I looked up to. Now it was me being the big brother, giving him my shoulder to lean on. His jive, his quick mouth, his playboy ways had vanished for the moment. Mookie was quiet and scared, wondering why all these terrible things had happened and what his future might hold.

I lost my own anger, and started to settle into a depression. Not surprisingly, I turned to basketball to unleash my feelings and get my mind off all the problems of friends and family. As a sophomore, I was in a position of leadership, and I still enjoyed great popularity with the fans. But there was a new crop of freshmen on the team, and they were cocky as ever, running and gunning wildly, even worse than we sophomores had done the year before. The team did not have that sense of closeness that we felt, and I missed that. As the leader, I wasn't sure what to do to get that feeling back; in the end, I decided to lead by example, playing as hard as I could, and letting the younger players learn their roles from Coach Stone.

Part of our problem is that we had "been to the mountaintop," as one sportswriter put it, and after you've won it all in such Cinderella fashion, it is very tough to gear up mentally to do it all again. The year before, we came back from disaster so many times that it seemed almost as if *it was meant to be* that we would win the championship. The title was a goal we wanted as a *team*, not as individuals. The players on this team, though, had their minds elsewhere.

One of the new freshmen was a hot-shooting guard from Alabama named Nate Bufford. He was very talented, but every time you gave him the ball, no matter where he was on the court or how many guys were guarding him, he took a shot. Fans have no idea how that demoralizes a team, even if the guy is hitting pretty well. There are five players on the court, and they all want to be involved. "Ball hogs" quickly alienate their teammates, and there was more than one group session about Mr. Bufford's shooting.

"That man is a Black Hole," said my roomie, Rodney McChriston. "You throw the ball in there, and it never comes back."

"It's a one-way trip, no doubt about that," offered Chester. "Spud, you got to quit dealing to the man."

"I hear you, Cheddar," I replied. "Next time I pass off to him, I'm just gonna take a seat on the bench until he's finished shooting, then I'll run back in and play D until we get the ball and give it back to Mr. Bufford."

In Nate Bufford's defense, a lot of good players find themselves on teams where they have to carry the scoring or rebounding load. As players graduate to better teams, they keep shooting and shooting even though there are talented support players alongside them. To some extent, it was that way for me at Wilmer Hutchins, and as a sophomore at Midland, with so much attention, there was some pressure to be everything the fans wanted, a player who could take over the game. At times, I loved being the center of attention, the quarterback who ran the game with an eye toward what it would take for my team to win. But the more I played, the more I enjoyed the *team* aspects of basketball: getting different players involved in the flow, passing off to the open man even when I had a wide-open shot, putting pressure on the other team's defense, waiting for them to make a mistake. I understood from experience: There's a lot to the game of basketball that a player right out of high school just doesn't know, and there are countless skills to be gained from playing with a *cohesive*, talented college team. I was still learning plenty from every game, but I was continually frustrated by the foolish play of some of our freshmen, who seemed to be out more for themselves than for the team.

I was part of the problem, because I was bringing my moods onto the court. I couldn't help it. So many terrible things had happened, and I withdrew from everybody into my own world. Over time, this attitude of "Stay away, world" must have gotten to Coach Stone, because before the holiday break, he told me to get a grip on myself. I hadn't told him all the things that had gone wrong.

Christmas was pretty lousy, with Dad in prison and Mookie still in a state of shock. Talking about basketball depressed him, because he knew he would never play competitively again. We talked about coaching, and how we'd both love to work with kids someday, and how we'd be better coaches than the ones we had growing up. My brothers and sisters were all working hard to keep the store running, so we didn't have any big present exchange. I did get to spend time with Dawn, which was nice, and she listened patiently as I talked about all my trials and tribulations. Ever since my dad moved out of the house, when I was a teenager, I had become used to having understanding women around me for support, so it was comfortable to have Dawn to talk to. She said she would visit Midland more often after the break.

Going back to school was hard and lonely. Midland was freezing, and sitting on a cold bench in the locker room before practice one day, I wondered about my basketball career, about whether there would be anything after this year or whether it would all end at this remote junior college 700 miles from anywhere.

I'm ashamed to say this, because I always prided myself on giving 100 percent, but I played some lackluster games. Finally, after one game that we barely won, Stone came up and really chewed me out.

"What's the matter with you, Spud?" he hollered. "You never talk to me! You'll talk to people on the street before you'll come to me. Now stop being so damn private and tell me what's going on with you!"

I started crying. I tried not to, but the grief just poured out of me as I told Coach Stone about my dad, about

Mookie, about my frustrations with the game and my worries about the future. I have always been a little suspicious of coaches, but Stone really cared and that talk helped a great deal to bring me back to life.

I also turned to the Bible for inspiration. Reverend Jenkins used to say, "Everything you need is in that Book, if you'll just read it with an open heart." I read Proverbs a lot, about wisdom and how God gives us wisdom to know which path we should take. I read about Job, a faithful servant of God who had everything taken away from him and yet he still trusted God and praised Him for all the blessings in his life. I realized I had a lot; I had a good mind, a loving family, good friends who cared about me, and, finally, a healthy body that could do incredible things. The Bible says, "Pray without ceasing," and I did—praying for everything from Mookie and his recuperating knee to the parole board that would hear my Dad's release case. Physically, I was in great shape; now I was on the road to getting mentally and spiritually in order as well.

I began to play better. Our team won our conference and went to the Regional Tournament once again. We lost, but it was a fine follow-up to our dream season the year before. I was named to the junior college All-American team, closing out a great career at Midland. Many people wrote letters to me, heartfelt, emotional letters saying how much they enjoyed seeing me play. Reading letters like that make me feel fantastic! I can't imagine anyone *ever* getting tired of reading fan mail.

I realize I haven't mentioned much about school, although I enjoyed my classes at Midland. I was studying criminal justice, the world of cops and robbers, and it was fascinating. When I was a little kid, I always loved detective shows, watching how the detectives use all these clues to figure out the crime, then catch the criminal when he makes a wrong move. TV detectives seemed also to be good, admirable guys who wanted to help people out, not just put crooks in jail. I wanted to be like that.

Most of the cops in Midland were pals of mine by my sophomore year, and when I had the chance I rode around in the squad car with them, talking police work and basketball. I saw them arrest a lot of drunks, and watched while people on drugs wept, vomited, and pleaded for more drugs. That, more than anything, made me certain I was never going to put any drugs in my body—and I never have.

For me, the best part of criminology is getting inside another person's mind, seeing what that person is thinking, and trying to predict what he's going to do. Police these days have sophisticated computers to determine tendencies of various criminals, but a lot of the work is still the good old-fashioned hunch. When my basketball career is finally over, I think some work in criminal justice would be interesting. In fact, one of my NBA friends, Karl Malone of the Utah Jazz, is a sheriff in the off-season in Louisiana and he says it is great work.

Out on the court, I sometimes try to use things I've learned about predicting what a man might do in a given situation. When you watch films, you see if a man has a tendency to go to his left or right, or how he sets himself to shoot. Playing defense, definitely the hardest part of basketball, means using your hunches and trying to beat your man to a certain spot on the floor where he wants to shoot or pass from. And don't think these NBA players don't have criminal tendencies: Take your eye off the ball for one second, and they'll steal you blind.

Summer was approaching, and once again I had some big decisions to make. Where would I be next year? I had a chance to visit several schools, but my ace-in-the-hole, North Texas State, was gloomy because Bill Blakeley had just been fired, even though he had the winningest record in NTSU history.

I knew one thing. I had confidence. My days at Midland had been exactly what I needed to hone my playing skills and give me a strong sense of my abilities. Had I gone to a four-year school to begin with, I probably wouldn't have started and I certainly would never have had the big-game pressure experience I got at Midland. Like I said, all there'd been to do was study and play hoops. What's more, I had a national championship under my belt, something most people can only dream of. I had worked hard, but I had also been lucky. I think the two go hand in hand. Now, looking for my next destination, I hoped to get lucky again. For one year, things had fallen apart, but now they were coming together again, and I was about to get luckier than I ever imagined.

9

"If That's Spud Webb, You're Fired!"

I'm sure a lot of guys would have been perfectly content with a basketball resumé that included a national junior college title. But I wanted more. That taste of success only made me hungrier to test myself against major college competition.

I was sure I was good enough. I'd proven myself. After what I'd accomplished, I viewed the next step on the basketball ladder as just another challenge. But would I get that chance? And who would provide it? A few schools showed interest, but the big-time Division I coaches remained skeptical.

When the recruiting mating dance was set in motion, I was disappointed that only schools like North Texas State, Southern Illinois, and Bradley seemed to have interest in me. NTSU was a logical option simply because it is in Denton, just north of Dallas. My family and friends from home would be able to jump in the car and attend my games.

I was surprised that not one Southwest Conference school offered me a scholarship. But I brushed the snub aside, reasoning that maybe it just went to show why the SWC will always be considered a football conference.

Then suddenly North Carolina State entered the picture. The defending NCAA champs needed a point guard. Badly. They had seriously courted Kenny Hutchinson, a guy I had read about. He was a blue-chip prospect from New York City, where NC State did a lot of its recruiting. I figured the only reason Coach Jim Valvano was even remotely interested in me was as a hedge in case Kenny decided to go elsewhere.

That's exactly what happened. Again, God smiled on me. Hutchinson's mother wouldn't let him sign early. Then he had a last-minute change of heart and signed with Eddie Sutton, who was head coach at the University of Arkansas. At the time I'd scheduled one more on-campus recruiting visit, to Oklahoma City University. Abe Lemons, the former University of Texas coach, was running the show at OCU and he favored a wide-open style that seemed to be ideally matched to my game. I always wanted to play for Abe. When he was at Texas, I wanted to play for him badly.

NC State assistant Tom Abatemarco called me on a Thursday night. He'd contacted Coach Stone a few days before and found out I hadn't yet signed a letter of intent. Later I learned that I was their last hope. If I had turned them down, the defending college basketball champs were going to enter the following season without a true point guard. Apparently Coach V (what the players called Valvano) was tied up for a full month after the Wolfpack beat the University of Houston for the title and he wasn't able to spend as much time recruiting as he normally liked. Abatemarco had investigated me without my knowing it. At this level a recruiter really has to do his homework on a player, especially when the target is shorter than your average cheerleader.

Tom remembered a story about me in *Sports Illustrated* written by a pretty good writer named Rick Telander. Telander said some flattering things about me, leading his story with a few humorous remarks about my nickname and with some quotes from my brother, David. Of course my height and jumping ability were prominently mentioned in the article and Abatemarco remembered that. Meanwhile, the State staff was busy making phone calls and computer checks, trying to get a line on me. Abatemarco later visited Midland, met with Stone, and picked up some tapes of our Midland College games from a local television station. He'd also watched me play in a few spirited pickup games at our gym. My schedule had no more open weekends for an additional recruiting visit but Abatemarco is a very persuasive fellow. I was used to dealing with low-key coaches, but he was like a whirlwind. I'm a very private person so I didn't say much during our phone conversation; however, I agreed to fly to Raleigh-Durham, North Carolina, to see the State campus and meet Coach V and Abatemarco.

When I got off the plane and walked into the departure lounge, there wasn't anyone there to greet me. I thought, "If they were so hot to meet me, where are they?" My plane had arrived at the wrong gate and they were in another part of the airport: still, it's not as though the Raleigh-Durham airport is the size of the Dallas–Fort Worth International or Chicago's O'Hare. I went to the baggage claim area and stared at the suitcases sliding down the chute. Had they decided they didn't want a 5'5" point guard after all? My head was swimming with awful possibilities.

Then I saw two Italian-looking guys in coats and ties. Both had longish dark hair, basic Beatle cuts. One had a mustache. So, I thought, these two crime bosses are going to be the men who would make a major imprint on the rest of my life? As I approached them, I saw the man with the mustache say something to his companion. The two of them laughed. Were they laughing at me? I was flushed with embarrassment. Later, they told me that the exchange went something like this:

Abatemarco: "Coach V, that's him. That's Spud."

Valvano: "Tom, if that kid in the jockey cap is Spud Webb, then you're fired!"

I must have looked like a lost little boy. And they said they'd had me paged, but I must not have heard it. Anyway, although I felt confident, my palm was sweating a little as we shook hands and did the introductions. Then we collected my bag and drove to the Wolfpack basketball offices at Case Athletics Center. I just stared out the window during the drive. I had to admit that it was pretty country, but I wasn't much for small talk. I let these two fast-talking New Yorkers handle the chore of conversation. But man, could these guys talk! If the subject wasn't basketball, then it was Italian food, with one always trying to outdo the other. The talk reminded me of the friendly woofing that used to go on in my old neighborhood—with different accents, of course.

At the athletics center we went directly to a screening room to watch films of the team from the previous season. Of course as a basketball fan I was well aware of people like Thurl Bailey, Derek Whittenburg, and Sidney Lowe, three of the graduating stars from the national champs. And who could forget Lorenzo Charles' slam dunk of Whittenburg's desperation shot at the buzzer, which gave NC State the title?

One of the Wolfpack opponents they showed me on film was Othell Wilson, the stocky Virginia point guard. Wilson was tougher than a cheap cut of steak. He wasn't big, although he was several inches taller than me. He'd get into your face and play great defense. "If you come here you'll be matched up against strong guys like this," Valvano said. "You're going to have problems on defense because of your size." I nodded politely, then made one of my rare pronouncements: "I may have problems with him. But I know for sure that he'd have problems with me."

And in the back of my mind I knew they were stuck for a point guard. Lowe, the team leader of the NCAA champs, was graduating. Kenny Hutchinson, once their savior, was going to be playing Wooo-Pig-Sooey for Eddie Sutton's Arkansas Razorbacks. Playing in the Atlantic Coast Conference really appealed to me. Basketball here was high-profile, with rabid fans and classy arenas and top coaches like Valvano, Dean Smith, Mike Krzyzewski, and Bobby Cremins. What's more, many of the defending champ's games would be on national television and on cable, meaning that the home folks would be able to see me play. ACC basketball was like the Cowboys in Dallas —bigger than life.

"So what do you think, Spud?" Valvano asked.

There's an expression that's popular with coaches: "There are no great people. There are just great opportunities." I knew this was mine, there for the taking, like a breakaway lay-up.

"I think you need me," I replied, without a hint of a boast.

Abatemarco took a trip to Midland to finish his Spud homework, and soon thereafter Valvano offered me a scholarship. He'd screened the videos and heard the glowing reports from Abatemarco, his top recruiter. It didn't take longer than a heartbeat for me to accept.

As soon as I said yes, Valvano strode into his office, a big smile painted across his face, and called several friends.

"I just signed our new point guard and he's 5′5″ tall," Coach V was saying with a laugh.

"You've finally lost it, V," went the usual response. "You mean you're going to replace Sidney Lowe, the all-time ACC assist leader and a block of granite besides, with a 130-pound shrimp named 'Spud'?"

"You're damned right," Valvano would say. "And wait till you see him. This kid is going to bring the house down."

I knew it wouldn't be a snap, yet it's difficult not to be enthused when you're around two men as positive and bubbly as Valvano and Abatemarco. Valvano was convinced that with good coaching he could channel my raw talent into the talent of a productive and perhaps spectacular college player. All I knew was I was getting my chance. It was up to me to do something with it.

As practices began that fall, there were a few snickers as I ran the offense the first couple of times. Here was this kid who looked as though he belonged in junior high calling the plays for the reigning national champs. But the jitters didn't last long and I made sure to distribute the ball to Lorenzo Charles, Cozell McQueen, and Terry Gannon. I'd get my shots later. My first priority was to blend in, keep my teammates happy, take care of business as a point guard. Fans and media flocked to our open workouts. I felt thousands of sets of eyes following my every move, waiting for me to make a mistake.

My biggest adjustment in that point guard role was being vocal, being Coach V's leader on the floor. In high school and at Midland I hadn't been a pure point guard. Oh, I did plenty of creative things with the ball that caused openings for my teammates. But I was depended upon for scoring. A true point guard looks to pass first and shoot as a secondary option.

Valvano's point guard also called all the defenses after they'd been relayed from the bench. The point man was the coach's presence on the court. Not only was I a naturally quiet, very private person, I also was jumping into a situation where I felt a little like an outsider, an interloper barging into this tight group of players, most of whom had been together since they were freshmen.

Sometimes I'd forget to tell my four teammates what defense we were playing. I didn't mean it. I'd just never played that role before. Coach V would get mad, but he didn't hold a grudge. That was the nicest thing about him, why guys would run through a flaming hoop for him. He was a regular guy, although a slightly wacko regular guy.

I also had to learn to pace myself. Previously I'd played at only one speed: overdrive. Valvano convinced me to tone my game down a bit, that my speed and quickness sometimes would get me in trouble. Coach V has always contended that my game was better suited to the pros than to college, which is why he soon became confident that I could make it in the NBA.

Coach V couldn't have scheduled a tougher opener if he'd buttonholed Red Auerbach and lined up the Celtics. Our honorable first-game opponent was the University of Houston in a rematch of the 1983 championship game.

Let's talk about pressure, in an industrial-sized tank.

We were in Springfield, Massachusetts, for the Hall of Fame Tip-Off Classic, the first big game of the season. Like any good basketball fan I knew that Dr. James Naismith invented the game in Springfield back in 1891. The city is crammed with history, much of it involved with my favorite game. Springfield is such a basketball town that there are peach baskets attached to some of the city's streetlights. (Naismith used peach baskets as the original hoop and cylinder.) The Basketball Hall of Fame is in Springfield, and since 1979 the game has served as the college season's springboard. In other words, what better place for a hoops junkie like myself to begin his big-time career?

NBC was counting on blockbuster television ratings, and this was the game to get them. The Houston Cougars, with talents like Akeem Olajuwon, Alvin Franklin, Michael Young, and Rickie Winslow, were here to prove on national television that their loss to State the previous March was simply an aberration. This was Phi Slamma Jamma, Texas' tallest fraternity, ranked in the top three on every national poll, not your customary first-game cannon fodder like Crabcake Tech or East Podunk State.

NBC-TV commentator Al McGuire really put the monkey on our backs. "This game should prove what a fluke last year's championship was for NC State," McGuire said in a pregame feature. Thanks, pal. As if the Cougars, a 10-point favorite, didn't have enough incentive against an unranked team beginning a rebuilding season!

Turning to the Wolfpack's new floor leader, McGuire even questioned my program weight of 135 pounds. "No way, even if he ate a bunch of bananas before the weigh-in," McGuire giggled.

The Springfield Civic Center was jammed, and quite honestly I was as jittery as I'd ever been before a big game. What if I gave a lousy performance? I might not ever recover. Any seed of doubt planted in the back of Coach V's mind might eventually sprout until I was permanently benched, written off as a wrong-headed experiment. I was probably thinking too much, but these things happen when you're terrified. As I stood in the lay-up line, all I could think was, "Let's get this game started." Once referee Jack Hannon tossed up the ball for the tip-off, much of my nervousness escaped like steam from the ears of a cartoon character.

Two hours later I was the talk of the college basketball

Above: *Easter Sunday, 1975. My brother Reg (left) and I give a hug to our little neighbor, Regginald Bullard.*

Left: *No, it's not the young Michael Jackson—I had lots of hair as a high school kid.*

I practiced my early dunks on a basket we hung inside *our garage!*

Left: *Playing junior college ball in Midland, I found the competition getting bigger. Still, I looked for a way to "rise above" my opponents.*

The 1982 NJCAA Champions—the Cinderella team. Bottom row: trainer Arnalso Carrasco, Justin Morrett, Chester Smith, Lance McCain, Jerome Crowe, David Thompson. Top row: trainer Pat Scribner, coach Jerry Stone, me, Puntus Wilson, Chuck Robinson, Rodney McChriston, and trainer Michael Hudson.

*Webb family. Top row: Renée, Bean (David, Jr.), my father, Stephanie. Seated: B.J. (nephew),
Janice, Reg, my mother, Amber (niece).* (Patrick O'Sullivan)

I battle Tyrone "Mugsy" Bogues for a ball in a 1984 game between NC State and Wake Forest.

Right: *Holding on after a dunk for the Atlanta Hawks.* (Mark Graham, Dallas Times Herald)

Below: *Going up for a dunk while at NC State.*

Me and my friend Manute Bol, the 7'7" center for the Washington Bullets, at a press conference.

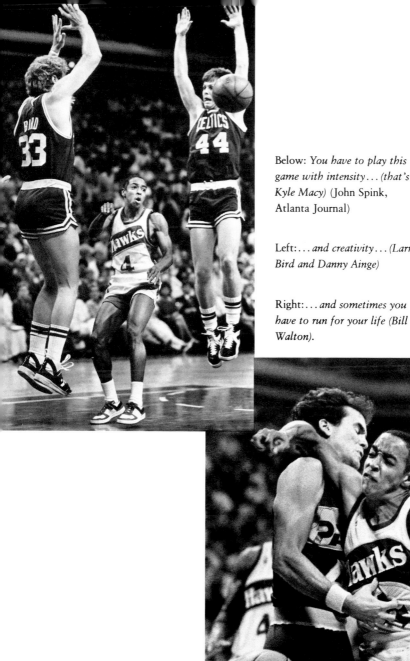

Below: *You have to play this game with intensity... (that's Kyle Macy)* (John Spink, Atlanta Journal)

Left: *... and creativity... (Larry Bird and Danny Ainge)*

Right: *... and sometimes you have to run for your life (Bill Walton).*

A quiet moment: reading mail in the locker room with Dominique Wilkins.

In Las Vegas with Larry Nance (left) of the Phoenix Suns, a good friend and one of the best forwards in pro basketball. In the middle is my pal Mike Tyson, to whom I'm always nice, since he's the Heavyweight Champion of the World.

Left: *A 360° reverse slam
helped me win the NBA Slam
Dunk Championship.* (Mark
Graham, Dallas Times Herald)

Below: *Fans showing their
appreciation, rating me a
"10"—plus some.* (Mark Graham, Dallas Times Herald)

Afterward I was interviewed by Bill Russell and Rick Barry. (Mark Graham, Dallas Times Herald)

Above: *A proud moment for me—being honored by the City of Atlanta and Mayor Andrew Young.*

Left: *Driving against Joe Dumars in the 1986 playoffs. I sank two free throws with three seconds left to win the game.*
(Robert Wachtel)

Coach Fratello tried to use my skills carefully. (Louie Favorite)

In the 1987 playoffs, I often had to guard Isiah Thomas. (Rich Addicks)

Being swarmed by teammates (at right is John Battle) after making the winning shot in the 1986 playoffs against Detroit to send the Hawks to the next round against the Celtics. (Rich Addicks)

world. Not only did we win, 76–64. That would have been enough for me. The personal garnish on this pressurized afternoon were my numbers on the final box score. I finished with 18 points, 5 assists, 4 rebounds, and 3 steals and was named the game's Most Valuable Player. I also made one pretty spectacular play, driving the length of the court and hitting a lay-up over Akeem, Mr. Phi Slamma Jamma himself. NBC was so impressed with the play that they used it all season as part of their basketball promo. The arena erupted and I could almost envision my friends at home dealing high-fives as they watched it on the tube.

Several people later made the observation that Houston wasn't prepared for my style of play. After the game, McGuire said, "No doubt about it, in a game which was supposed to be a battle of two big, strong teams, the difference was tiny Spud Webb. This kid is amazing!"

That wasn't exactly the word I would have used to describe myself that afternoon. "Relieved" would have been a better choice. All the kind words were flattering, but it was only the third week in November. The season had almost four months to run. Still, the victory felt wonderful. This time nobody could label the result a fluke. "We were soundly outplayed," Houston coach Guy V. Lewis said later.

Houston had failed against us in the championship game in Albuquerque because the Cougars failed to convert pressure free throws and because they couldn't stop NC State's long-range shooting. Can you say "déjà vu"? The Cougars made only 3 of 12 free throws in the second half. And we were on fire from the outside. I made 7 of my 11 field goal attempts. Terry Gannon nailed 5 of 9. Lorenzo Charles buried 7 of 11. I fouled out with about 5 minutes left, but by then we'd built an 11-point lead.

"Spud really ignited us," Coach V told the reporters outside our locker room. "I wasn't sure how our ballclub would react to him. We tried to concentrate on defense and keep it simple."

Then we were on the road again, to a corner of the globe not reachable by bus. One of Valvano's selling points was that by joining NC State I'd have a chance to see other parts of the country. I hadn't traveled much, mostly in Texas and the Southwest. So I was excited about playing in the Great Alaskan Shootout, a tournament used by many of the top coaches to fine-tune their squads for the season.

If there was any chance of my developing a big head based on my work in the Houston game, I got a dose of reality in our first two assignments of the Shootout. I averaged 4.5 points and totaled 5 assists in victories over Alaska-Anchorage and Santa Clara. But in the championship game we beat 14th-ranked Arkansas, 65–60. I had 13 points, 10 assists, and 3 steals. I also ran the offense the way I had against Houston. "Spud finally took charge and penetrated and did some of the things we wanted him to do," Valvano said.

Still, it was entirely too early to start making reservations for the Final Four. A reporter asked Coach V if we could repeat as national champions. "Are you kidding?" he said, opening his eyes wide for dramatic effect. "Sometimes it's hard enough for us to get on the bus."

Nevertheless, we'd beaten two nationally ranked teams in 10 days. What I especially enjoyed about the victories was that they came against two Southwest Conference teams, neither of whom thought I could play major college ball. Following a 19-point blowout of North Carolina–Charlotte in the first round of the McDonald's Classic at Greensboro, North Carolina, however, we received what became the first in a series of lessons in humility. Led by future NBAer Dell Curry's 25 points, Virginia Tech handed us an 89–65 thrashing.

We finally played a home game, 20 days after our season opener, and we were anxious to put on a show for the locals. We overwhelmed Western Carolina, 82–61, and I had a decent game with 10 points, but I only contributed 3 assists, not exactly what I had in mind. Because of our victories over Houston and Arkansas we'd risen from being unranked to being number 8 in the country, according to the AP poll. Coach V wasn't thrilled with the extra attention.

"We really don't need that kind of pressure," he said. "We're just trying to improve. We're not nearly as bad as some people thought, and we're not nearly as good as our early-season victories seemed to indicate. We're somewhere in between. We're still a youthful team."

December 7 was a special night for another reason. Our national championship banner was raised in the pregame ceremonies; with the NCAA title banner from 1974, State now had a pair of them. Even though I had nothing to do with the win in '83, I felt good for teammates like Lorenzo Charles and Terry Gannon, guys who had experienced that storybook season. I had a fair notion of that feeling, however, from my time at Midland.

Three days later we smothered Hofstra, 82–56, and I was able to demonstrate to the Reynolds Coliseum faithful some of the high-wire abilities they'd been reading about me. Twice in the second half I stole the ball and went in for breakaway solo dunks. I discovered that Carolina fans weren't much different from the fans who'd backed me in Dallas and Midland. The crowd went absolutely nuts.

As anyone who knows me will tell you, I love to dunk. A slam at the proper moment in a game can lift the crowd's emotions. A dunk also can boost your teammates, get their juices flowing after a lethargic spell. But at State I didn't want to be known strictly as a dunk-master. (I still

115

don't.) In Raleigh it was always a struggle to be recognized for my all-around game.

I was experiencing problems meshing with Coach V's system. We weren't what you would call a perfectly matched pair. There were times during my two years at State when I was convinced Neil Simon must have written *The Odd Couple* with Coach and me in mind. Because I was the quarterback, Coach V wanted to talk to me during every time-out to plot strategy. And strategy is what separates the college and pro games. Even with the introduction of the shot clock, college hoops hinges on two key elements: time and score. As an instinct player, a freelancer, there were games and practices when I drove the coaches nuts. When I saw an opening, I'd take it, even when strategy would dictate the wisdom of laying back. Coach Stone had improved my skills immensely as a team leader, but I still had much to learn.

I was taken to school in the following game, another one of those nationally televised extravaganzas. We'd risen to 6th on the poll. Perennial power Louisville was rated 16th and the game was at Reynolds.

This time the lesson came on defense and I was powerless to do much about my plight. We lost, 83–79, because Louisville's Denny Crum did a masterful coaching job. Crum's offense was designed to work guards Lancaster Gordon, Milt Wagner, and Jeff Hall along the baseline. Since I'm 5′6″ and Terry Gannon is 6′0″, the scheme had merit. The idea was to post us up and shoot little jump shots over us. Gordon is 6′3″, Wagner is 6′5″, and Hall is 6′4″. No matter that I have a remarkable vertical leap, all three are good athletes and could get the shots off over me. Gordon had 25 points, Wagner, 20, and Hall, 12 off the bench. The reason I congratulate Crum for his coaching is not so much because of the plan itself. A high school coach could have suggested it. But so often the players will basically ignore their coach's pregame report: In this case, when Crum talked, the right people listened.

My offensive numbers were respectable: 15 points, 10 assists. But defensively I was concerned that I'd be singing a lot more of the post-op blues in the ACC season. I also learned the value of experience. Louisville was a veteran team and the Cardinals kept their cool, even with 12,400 partisan Wolfpack maniacs screaming at them.

"I think our team kept its composure," Wagner said. "We just executed our game and tried to calm the crowd down."

I made a few offensive errors that cost us that afternoon. In the second half Crum slapped on a 2-2-1 zone press. I'd encountered it before and knew the way to beat it was by passing the ball. But I went into my Marques Haynes act and tried to burn the press by dribbling. Against a good team like Louisville that's pure folly and I lost the ball several times.

Now it was time to start pointing toward the ACC season. We finished off 1983 with easy victories over North Carolina A & T, Towson State, and Campbell College. I was in a slump, with two points and seven assists against A & T and only two assists against Towson. I also received a scare in the Campbell game when I injured my ankle in the first half but I was back in the lineup during the second half.

Even though we were 9–2 entering conference play, the sportswriters still labeled us a mystery team. We'd been impressive enough in tough games against Houston and Arkansas; on the other side of the ledger were a total humiliation at the hands of Virginia Tech and a defeat to a good Louisville team. There were some positive signs. I was getting acquainted with my new teammates. Ernie

117

Myers, a 6'5" shooting guard with loads of talent, was working his way into the substitution pattern. And Lorenzo Charles was blossoming into an outstanding player.

Then, briefly, the world came crashing down around my ears. For a time the coaching staff must have wished they'd left me in the Raleigh-Durham airport at our first meeting.

We opened the season at home against Maryland before the usual packed house. And the Terps laid a 59–55 knot on our skulls. I was awful: 2 points, 1-for-7 shooting, 2 assists, and only 18 minutes on the floor. Ugh! Three days later we drew an even stiffer assignment: North Carolina with a lineup of future first-round draft picks that included Michael Jordan, Sam Perkins, Brad Daugherty, and Kenny Smith, with Joe Wolf coming off the bench. Pack up that bunch, pay the franchise fee, and you'd win yourself a lot of games in the NBA. With the national television cameras on us for the third time that season, we were soundly beaten, 81–60. Perkins, the future Dallas Maverick star, had 22 points. Jordan, the one-man show, sure to be the NBA MVP sometime in the future, had 18 points and 12 rebounds. My play had been so spotty against Maryland that I didn't even start against the Tar Heels. Myers and Gannon went most of the way in the backcourt. I played only 10 minutes.

Two days later we fell to 0–3 in the ACC, losing to Clemson on the road, 63–61. I was back among the regulars, teaming at guard with Myers, but the results weren't much better.

"I went back to what was working at the beginning of the year, with Spud in there from the start," Coach V said afterwards. "Ernie [Myers] doesn't play well off the bench and Spud hasn't been either."

Things were getting ugly. We lost at Virginia by three and were drop-kicked by nine by Georgia Tech at Atlanta. Last year's champs were 0–5 in the ACC, the numbers that mattered most to our fans, and I wasn't helping matters. I had two assists against Virginia, and Othell Wilson, the tough point guard Valvano had shown me on film a few months earlier, was all over me as I contributed only two assists against Tech.

The Georgia Tech defeat was probably the low point of the season. We shot a chilly 20 of 61 from the field. "We couldn't put the ball in the ocean," said Valvano, not exaggerating all that much. The Wolfpack hadn't lost five in a row since 1966–67, when they dropped eight straight.

This was a very lonely time for me. I kept to myself, preferring to stay in my room and write letters to my family and friends and my girlfriend. I wondered whether I had underestimated the adjustments one must make to jump from junior college to the ACC. Maybe it would have been easier to move from high school directly to major college ball rather than from high school to junior college to ACC. I don't know. Obviously I had no choice. This was the way it had to be.

I roomed with Bennie Bolton. Bennie spent his own amount of time in Coach V's doghouse, shuttling in and out of the starting lineup. Lorenzo Charles and Cozelle McQueen were also good friends of mine. Actually, I got along with everyone. I'm just not much of a social butterfly. Whenever the guys would try to pry me out of my room to go drinking or cruising, I'd beg off. Everybody has their own methods of relaxing. I preferred to either write letters or burn up the phone lines to Texas. I also spent a lot of time studying. I was never what you would call a bookworm, but some of my courses, particularly those in criminolgy and education, held my interest.

Mail call was among my favorite times of the day. Frances Lewis, Coach V's long-time secretary, would make sure I'd get my mail. Much of it was from young fans, small kids who like me had been told to take up a sport other than basketball. Those letters always lifted my spirits. Mrs. Lewis once told me I'd become the number-one request for autographed pictures. Just then Coach V walked into the office.

"Now, I've got only one rule here, Spud," Valvano said with that big grin of his. "Nobody can be more popular than the coach."

I smiled back. "Well, then, coach," I replied. "I suggest you work on perfecting your dunk shot."

Coach V and the guys would kid me about my shyness. Valvano once joked that I was attending school on a Marcel Marceau Scholarship.

Reeling from a losing streak, what our team needed was an old-fashioned rout to break the tension and get us back on track. Luckily, University of North Carolina–Wilmington was just what the doc ordered. We won in a walk, 81–53, and I had 11 points (5-of-6 from the field) and 7 assists.

"After those five tough losses—three of them really tough losses, too, ones we thought we had a shot at—we just needed this," Valvano said. "When you lose five in a row, any 'W' comes at a good time." Three days later we went out and collected our first ACC "W" of the season.

The Wake Forest Deacons came to Reynolds and they were the cure for what ailed us. We brushed them aside, 80–69. I finally broke loose from the slump that had me by the throat: 18 points, 13 assists and an 8-for-8 performance from the free-throw line. Talk about relieved!

We'd been really dragging during the bad spell and we approached the Wake Forest game like it was a crusade. "We really needed this one," my man "Lo" Charles told the press. "We're trying to get another NCAA bid and we figure we have to be seven–seven in the conference. We have five [ACC] games left in our gym and our plan is to try and win all five at home and sneak in two wins on the road." Lorenzo had 23 points and 12 rebounds and the reporters continued to lob questions at him. "The key for us was that we were very emotional and intense for a span of twenty minutes," he said. "We've been fired up for our other games, but we'd only sustain it for thirty-five minutes. That's why we lost some tough games. We have to keep on plugging. Last year we were nine–seven at one point but kept on plugging, kept on trying hard. That's what we plan on doing this year."

In a way Lo was throwing a challenge at my feet. If we were to keep that fire in our bellies for the entire 40 minutes of a game, the task would be mine as floor leader to maintain that sharp edge. For me the Wake Forest game was significant from another aspect. I got my first look at a guy to whom I have been compared by even the most casual fan. Tyrone "Mugsy" Bogues, the Deac's 5'3" reserve point guard, played six minutes without a point or an assist. But I certainly recognized another bundle of talent in a small package. Mugsy and I would seriously get it on my senior year.

I had 29 points and 20 assists in our back-to-back victories and for that I was named ACC Rookie of the Week. In addition, I was leading the conference in assists, so despite all my struggles I must have been doing something right.

We were hard-pressed to edge The Citadel, 50–49, at Charlotte. A very talented player named Regan Truesdale put up 25 points for The Citadel and I was very nearly the goat of the game. We were leading, 49–47, with two and a half minutes left and I was fouled. But I missed the free throw. Cozelle McQueen bailed me out with a rebound, but I was called for a charge and The Citadel had the ball back with 1:09 to play. Truesdale missed again and with 28 seconds to play Russell Pierre hit a free throw to bump our lead to 50–47. The Citadel missed two shots on its next possession and I was fouled when we got the ball back. With a chance to assure victory, I messed up again, missing the free throw. Truesdale got another bucket and we were barely able to hold on for the victory.

While our performance was far from artistic, it was another of those "Ws" we'd gone so long without. We weren't about to turn back. We caught ourselves another breather, beating up on Furman, 95–72. I made all my shots, 4 from the field, 4 from the line for 12 points to go with my most important category, assists. I had 11.

My education as a big-time point guard was ongoing. I never thought of myself as a gunner or a ball hog but wherever I'd played before, my job was to score points in bunches. With this group, there were plenty of guys who could put the ball in the hole. I was on the floor to set them up.

Our next game gave me the distinct feeling we were on a roll. We beat Clemson, 69–59, at Reynolds in one of Lo's best games. In spite of double- and sometimes triple-team attention, Lorenzo had 23 points, 14 in the second half, to help us pull away in the final 5 minutes. I was satisfied with my game: 10 points, 11 assists. We'd now won three straight in the ACC and we were feeling a lot better about ourselves.

The next game would present an even stiffer test: Georgia Tech, with Mark Price, John Salley, and Bruce Dalrymple. Tech was a reflection of Coach Bobby Cremins, a hustling, scrappy team. Like Coach V, Cremins was a product of the New York City schoolyards. Put Valvano and Cremins together and their accents are thicker than the crust on Sicilian pizza. We managed to squeeze out a 68–67 triumph, again because Lorenzo took charge with 26 points. Lo set the tone early when he powered his way inside, threw down a thunderous stuff, was fouled, and converted a free throw only 50 seconds after the opening tap.

That play got us pumped and got the Reynolds Coliseum rabble into the game early. We'd won our eighth straight, improving our ACC record to 4–5 and our overall mark to 18–7. Twenty-plus victories seemed a safe bet and we thought that kind of record would sew up an NCAA bid. Another factor in our favor was our status as defending tournament champions.

Coach V warned us against overconfidence against our next opponent, Northeastern. It would be difficult not to overlook Northeastern because our archrival, North Carolina, loomed as our next conference assignment, at Chapel Hill, no less. Even our fans were looking past Northeastern. During the game, many in the Reynolds Coliseum crowd of 11,000 chanted, "Bring on Carolina." Psychologically we felt the same way because the victory wasn't cinched until Terry Gannon hit a pair of free throws with six seconds to play, to bump our lead to 77–72.

The final was 77–74. The key for us was the defensive job we did on Northeastern star Reggie Lewis, who finished with 12 points, converting only 6 of 17 field goal attempts.

From one point of view I had a monster game, handing out 18 assists to tie the school record. Many of those setups went to Myers, who was red-hot from the field, scoring 32 points. However I wasn't at all pleased with the fact that I made only one of my seven shots from the floor and finished with four points.

"I said all along this would be a nail-biter and that's what it was," Valvano told the reporters. He sure was right. Of course Coach V was telling us that every game was going to be a nail-biter. All coaches do that and so often players don't listen. Sometimes you get the feeling coaches are only crying wolf when they say some of the things that they do.

So there we stood with a nine-game winning streak, feeling pretty cocky. The flip side was that the Carolina game was only three days off and the Tar Heels were on a roll of frightening proportions—it had lasted the entire season. They were ranked number one by both wire service polls, owned a 21–1 record, and were 9–0 in the ACC. Wake Forest and Duke were second, but a distant second at 5–4. Making things even stickier for us was the fact that Carolina had absorbed its first defeat of the season five days before, to Arkansas. We knew we were in for a war.

The Tar Heels let us know how tough they were going to be in the opening four minutes when they made a 15–4 run. We were down, 20–6, before we finally cleared our heads and figured out how to beat Carolina's double-team traps. We made one strong push to slash their lead to 30–24.

We trailed by 10 at halftime. Carolina spurted again early in the second half and the deficit was 24. We had one more rally left. I hit six quick points and we dragged UNC's advantage down to 19. But Michael Jordan was truly amazing, living up to his reputation as the nation's finest player. Defensively we opened with a 1-3 zone and decided to switch to a 2-3 zone, but against a talent like Jordan your only defense is a well-aimed baseball bat between his eyes. He constantly got inside our zone and scored 32 points, shooting 12-for-18, mostly on those soft fall-away jumpers he's still nailing in the NBA. We were trounced, 95–71. Our streak was over.

Individually, I had nothing to complain about. For one of the few times during the season, the team needed me to shoot. I was happy to oblige, hitting 10 of 12 shots and leading the team with 22 points. The crowd at Carmichael

Auditorium saved their most vocal responses for Jordan and me. We were involved in one play, with about two minutes to go in the game, that really set the crowd buzzing. Michael drove to the hoop and I was determined to stop him. The fans booed lustily as I was called for the foul, my fifth. But like good fans, they also gave me a nice ovation as I left the floor.

From that point on our season fell apart like a paper bag in the rain. We hosted Duke and got beat, 73–70. It's not as though the Blue Devils kicked us in the pants. Dan Meagher, an unspectacular post player, knocked down a pair of free throws with three seconds left in overtime to cinch the victory. Meagher almost beat us in regulation when he threw a 20-footer at the buzzer. But referee Dan Woolridge ruled that Meagher released the ball after time had expired. There were a lot of people in Reynolds Coliseum who thought otherwise.

I had a shot at being a hero. With the game tied at 68-all and about 10 seconds remaining in overtime, I drove the lane and put up a 12-foot off-balance bank shot that glanced off the side of the rim. Duke got the ball back and Russell Pierre fouled Meagher, who drove the two stakes into our hearts. We certainly missed Charles, who was shackled by foul problems and eventually fouled out, finishing with 11 points. I had 12 points and 12 assists but made only 6 of 14 from the field.

Time was growing short for us to fatten up our record and clinch the NCAA tournament spot that was now our principal goal. Obviously the rest of the conference had already conceded the regular-season crown to the Tar Heels. We didn't want to be in a situation where we had to win the conference tournament in order to assure an invite.

Our quest for our 20th victory was still within the realm of possibility. With two ACC games left, including our home finale, plus the tournament, surely we could scare up one victory! Coach V said we'd need "another win or two" to reach the NCAA field of 64.

We drew a blank. It was like going to Vegas and getting clobbered at blackjack, craps, and roulette, then taking the rest of your pocket change and feeding it to the slot machines.

Virginia got us first, 74–63. Othell Wilson had a super game with 24 points and 10 assists. Quite honestly, we were out of gas. Everyone was dragging, feeling the effects of the disappointing overtime loss to Duke. I had 11 points and 4 assists. Lorenzo Charles and Myers led us with 12.

"I guess the Duke game took a lot out of us, but that's no excuse," Valvano said. "The juices just weren't flowing." We knew we were digging ourselves deeper and deeper into a hole.

Maryland was next and the Terps struck us with another crippling blow, 63–50. I had six points and three rebounds, another spotty performance.

The regular season would end at Wake Forest. With our five-game losing streak, prospects seemed dim. We played well offensively, shooting a little better than 50 percent. But we couldn't stop the Deacs' offense and we got into foul problems. I picked up five personals. So did Cozelle and Ernie. I led the team with 19 points and 8 assists but those numbers had a hollow ring.

We had a week to get ready for the tournament, but with a five-game losing streak we weren't entering under ideal circumstances. As the seventh seed we had the misfortune of drawing second-seeded Maryland as our first-round opponent.

We gave them a run for their money before falling, 69–63. We trailed most of the way but rallied to within four points with a little less than two minutes left. However, we were forced to foul to stop the clock, and Maryland converted six of seven free throws over the final minute and a half.

That was it. The tournament was over for us and realistically we didn't have even a glimmer of hope of defending our NCAA title. We left the floor at Greensboro Coliseum that Friday night with an empty feeling. Coach V was as disappointed as any of us, but he kept his sense of humor. That's the only thing Valvano is never without. Also, Coach V would never criticize any of us in public, unlike a lot of coaches.

"I should have known it was going to be a tough day when I couldn't get in the building for an interview I was supposed to do this morning," Valvano said. "I guess that's the difference that a year makes. I'm proud of our kids. They were playing their brains out. We've lost six in a row, but five of them were to people probably going to post-season play."

Now we had to wait until Sunday afternoon to find out if we'd get an NIT bid. Quite frankly, we were a lock. With the NCAA field having been expanded to a fat 64, any big-name school with a winning record and some warm bodies in the starting lineup could make the NIT field.

Still, it would give us a last chance to salvage something from that wacky season. On Sunday a member of the NIT committee called Coach V and informed him we'd be playing Florida state, a Metro Conference member with a 19–10 record. At least we'd be playing at Reynolds. Our history of sellouts and enthusiastic crowds convinced the committee to schedule the game in Raleigh rather than at Florida State's arena in Tallahassee.

I guess our season ended in appropriate fashion. Coach V was excited about the prospect of playing in the NIT finals in his hometown, New York City, but you have to win three early-round games to get that far. We ended up

127

in overtime with Florida State: I thought we were about to take control when I canned a pair of free throws (two of my seven points) with a little over two minutes to go in the extra session, for a 71–70 lead. But with 40 seconds left Randy Allen hit a reverse lay-up and the Seminoles had the lead for good. Terry Gannon and Ernie Myers found openings for a pair of jump shots but neither one would fall, then a guy named Maurice Myrick threw down a dunk at the end to close us out. Another in the series of games we had every chance to win: And the final in over-time is Florida State, 74, NC State, 71. So much for our trip to the Big Apple.

I'll always be haunted by one last-second play in the game that directly led to our demise. I had my hands on the ball in the backcourt after intercepting a Florida State tip. The next thing I remember was being mugged and knocked to the floor by Myrick, who grabbed the ball and went in for his slam while I was flat on my back. I couldn't believe it! The no-call was criminal, but that's the way things went for us all during our losing streak.

Terry Gannon probably summed up our feelings best. "Once you've been to the top of the mountain, know how it feels, it's different," he said. "Now all we can do is watch the rest, those who don't have to put the ball away until next year. I don't know if I can watch or not, because I know how good that feels."

What a crazy season it was. At one point we were 10–2 and ranked seventh in the nation. Later we lost five straight conference games. Then we went on another ram-page, winning nine in a row. But after February 15 we didn't win another game, dropping seven straight. Talk about your streaky teams! We were the ultimate up-and-down club.

We all knew when the season began that it would be a shakedown cruise, a time of transition. Too many key elements from the championship team had graduated. That may be the biggest difference between college and pro basketball. The core of a great pro team might stay together for five or six seasons but a college program must fall back and regroup every couple of years.

When we started so quickly, the media figured Coach V had been hiding in the weeds, that his poor-mouthing was merely a ploy to lull our opponents into a false sense of security. On the contrary, his guarded preseason outlook turned out to be right on the money.

Adding to our woes had been the difficulty of our schedule. We played 16 games against NCAA-bound teams and 3 against clubs headed for the NIT. Our record against those tournament teams was 8–11.

The season was especially frustrating for Lorenzo. Teams usually collapsed two and sometimes three defenders around him. Even so, Lo led the ACC in scoring throughout much of the season before finishing with an 18.3 average, plus 8.5 rebounds. Those numbers earned him a spot on the All-Conference team.

As for me, I learned a lot and improved as a floor leader. I led the ACC in assists with 193 and averaged 9.9 points per game. I was far from satisfied, but I departed our postseason meeting anxious for my senior season.

First, however, Coach V would again deliver on that recruiting promise of travel opportunities. We were entered in a summer tournament in Greece that would offer not only basketball but educational growth.

All 14 members of the team made the trip, which lasted a week. First, we participated in a tournament with three other Greek teams in Thessaloniki. The only team to come close to us was Aris, which we beat 74–70, and we easily won the title. Competition got a lot stiffer in our final game and we lost to the Greek National A team, 77–73. Terry Gannon emerged as our scoring star in the four games with 60 points, 24 against a Greek A team. Lorenzo had 55 points and was named MVP of the tournament.

Coach V made sure we learned a little about Greek culture and history. A State professor, Dr. John Riddle, accompanied us and lectured us on what we were seeing; and a lot of the history that can seem so boring in the classroom suddenly came alive: The ancient Greeks seem a lot more interesting when you're standing on the steps of the Parthenon.

The tour also gave me a chance to get to know Nate McMillan, a transfer from Chowan Junior College in North Carolina, who'd grown up in Raleigh. Nate was a real talent and the plan was for him to join me in the backcourt, filling the role as the shooting guard.

Entering my senior season, hopes were high that we would challenge for the ACC title. That made sense because we had five returning starters, plus Nate, among our first eight players. Coach V had also done a good recruiting job in bagging Quentin Jackson, a point guard from DeMatha in Maryland, plus Vinny Del Negro, a shooter from Springfield, Massachusetts. Our biggest recruiting prize, however, was 6'11" Chris Washburn. Chris was a fine shooter for a big man and we looked to him to take a lot of the inside pressure off Lorenzo. One magazine even picked us to win the title. Just what we needed! More pressure.

Over the summer I kept working at the skills I'd been developing at point guard. I'd made progress the previous year, but I needed to be more consistent, to be more vocal running the show for Coach V.

Instead of drawing a bear like Houston, we opened against Campbell and we were an easy 95–54 winner. We also beat California–Santa Barbara, 73–70, and Hartford, which was making a jump into Division I competition,

83–46. Hartford's Hawks had a lot of heart, but we had a lot more talent.

We finished our preconference schedule with routs of North Carolina A & T and Western Carolina. We were ranked 10th in the nation by the AP—very flattering but serving only to heap more pressure on us.

My role had really changed. No longer was I a starter. In an effort to put more height in the lineup, Nate McMillan and Ernie Myers were starting along with a tall-trees frontcourt comprised of 6'9" Lorenzo Charles, 6'11" Chris Washburn, and 6'11" Cozell McQueen. I was the second or third player coming off the bench and while I wasn't totally pleased with the situation, I couldn't argue with the results. Because of the size of our frontcourt, we weren't able to run as much as we had the previous year. We were more of a halfcourt setup offensive team and that fact limited my effectiveness. My assignment was to get things done in the time I was out there. Then when the starters were back in, the opposing defense would have another adjustment to make. I had to trust in God that Coach V knew what was best for me and the team.

Our ACC opener was at home against Georgia Tech and we lost it, 66–64. Mark Price, considered a "little man" at 6'0", hit the game-winner, a 21-point jumper with one second left. My game wasn't much, with two points and three assists.

Our problem was we didn't maintain our intensity for the entire 40 minutes, the very thing Coach V was always preaching to us. I know the sportswriters consider intensity to be a cliché but it is a very important part of a player's performance. Ease up just the least bit against a high-quality team like Georgia Tech and you'll pay for it. "We let down just a tiny bit and that allowed Tech to come back," Lo said. Exactly.

We got another schedule break and took advantage of it, blasting St. Francis, 82–64. I played only eight minutes and had four points and one assist.

Now we were off for another of those exciting trips Coach V had promised. We were headed for his backyard, playing in the Holiday Festival at New York City's Madison Square Garden. New York's quite a place, although it isn't my style.

Controversy swirled around the team as we began the tournament. Chris Washburn had been dismissed from the team after he was arrested on a charge of second-degree burglary stemming from an incident at our athletic dorm. Coach V had no choice but to dismiss him.

Washburn's departure affected Lo most of all. Teams would again collapse their defenses around him. But a tighter player rotation also meant more playing time for me.

Our first tournament game was against a pretty decent Rutgers team. The game meant a lot to Coach V because Rutgers is his alma mater. I quickly found out how many extra minutes I was to inherit. Although I didn't start, I was on the floor for 37 minutes in our 80–68 victory. I had 16 points, hit 7 of my 13 shots, and had 7 assists, 5 steals, and, believe it, 7 rebounds.

The New York City papers and fans really took to me. But we were paired against the powerful team from Jamaica, Queens, fifth-rated St. John's, in the finals, and obviously we were a very different team without Chris. "We miss Chris on offense," Valvano said after the Rutgers game. "We're back to the same team as last year. We don't have the depth. In adversity clubs tend to come together and pull together. Whether it'll translate into wins and losses, I don't know."

Meanwhile, Rutgers coach Tom Young had paid me a nice compliment when he told the writers, "A lot of people may think I'm wacky but I'd rather see Washburn than Webb getting more playing time."

St. John's would be no picnic, especially with all the local fans solidly behind them. We knew we'd have a few people in our corner too, though, because Lo, Ernie Myers, and Russell Pierre were all from the area.

Coach V shook up the starting lineup. I was back with the first team and Russell also became a starter, replacing Terry and Ernie. I didn't play very well, failing to score, missing all four shots. I did have 4 assists in 18 minutes but the Johnnies whipped us, 66–56. It was obvious that their top three players, Chris Mullen, Walter Berry, and Bill Wennington, were all excellent pro prospects and as it turned out they are all in the NBA.

Our main problem was cold shooting. We hit only 37 percent from the field and the guys in the backcourt made only 5 of our 30 shots. It's hard to win with that kind of shooting from your guards. The game was a major disappointment, especially because we failed to win in front of Coach V's family and friends.

We didn't have much time to brood. That's one thing about basketball. No matter how bitter the defeat, you can't dwell on it because there's usually another game a few days away. Up next was our second ACC game, against Maryland and Lenny Bias at College Park in our first action of the new year, 1985.

Our slump continued as we were edged by the Terps, 58–56. It was like the previous season all over again. We had all sorts of opportunities to pull the game out but the breaks didn't go our way. Terry Gannon had a shot at tying the game with 4 seconds left but his 20-footer knocked off the front of the rim. We couldn't blame Terry. We all had our chances. I hit four of eight shots for eight points and had five assists but looking back I guess I could have done more.

Bias was certainly an impressive player. He led his team with 17 points, but the thing that really caught your eye about him was his smoothness. Those memories flashed through my head when I learned he was dead of a cocaine overdose. A chill came over me as I remembered his incredible moves on the court, and I couldn't imagine anyone gambling so much talent for the sake of drugs. All I can figure is that Lenny had no idea of the damage drugs would do to him.

A scan of the ACC standings in the paper the next morning found the Wolfpack in the cellar with an 0–2 record. Here people were picking us to win the title and we were in last place. Our slump had coincided with the departure of Chris Washburn. It was taking a while for us to adjust.

There would be no time for this squad to catch its breath, for we were immediately facing a nonconference contest against the University of Kentucky. And the Wildcats, playing before their home fans at Lexington, blasted us, 78–62. I was only 3-of-8 from the field and had 8 points but my 11 assists helped us to pull to within 6 points before the Wildcats spurted at the end.

Our biggest trouble was turnovers. We had 25 of them, while Kentucky was guilty of only 10. Also, the 'Cats made 34 of 37 free throws while we were talking only 17, converting 10. Home cooking? You be the judge. Valvano was most concerned with the turnovers and he pointed his finger at the guards. "Technically," he said, "the problem is in the backcourt."

It was crunch time, time to find out the size of our hearts. Virginia was our next assignment and guess who was back on the bench? I played only 16 minutes but they were productive minutes as I came up with 8 points to aid our win, 51–45. Terry also had a major role in the victory. He came off the bench to score 10 points, meaning that the reserve guards accounted for better than a third of our points. It was a relief to get our first ACC win.

We were back on the road, this time against Clemson, and we won our second in a row, 71–68. When Clemson pulled to within a point, we showed some of the determination we had perhaps lacked in previous close losses. Nate hit a pair of jumpers to pad our lead, then it was my turn to take the stage. With about three minutes left Coach V shifted us into a deliberate offense to take time off the clock. I ran the show, scored on a spinning drive, and finished with 10 points. Clemson crept back to within a point, but Lo canned a pair of free throws to close the Tigers out and even our ACC record at 2–2.

Now we faced our nemesis, North Carolina, at Chapel Hill. We came out with guns blazing and 3 minutes into the second half our lead had stretched to 15. With 11 minutes to go we were still up, 58–48.

Suddenly our offense stopped functioning. Carolina scored 14 unanswered points and the Tar Heels did not trail again in the game. Lorenzo had been switched from low post to a wing position and he'd gone wild, scoring 33 points. Two of those came when he converted an alley-oop pass from me, which turned out to be one of the most spectacular plays of the season. I had 10 assists and 9 points in 31 minutes. But those last 11 minutes did us in —Carolina took the win, 86–76.

We beat Florida State, the team that knocked us out of the NIT the previous spring, 72–66, and I was really getting comfortable with my bench role. I had 10 points, hitting 4 of 6 shots, and added a team-high 7 assists. We had a hard time concentrating on Florida State because a big ACC game awaited, against Duke at Reynolds Coliseum.

We ran away from the Blue Devils, 89–71, and I had a

super game, scoring 18 with 9 assists and 5 steals. Our ACC record was 3–3 and we were back into what was developing into a very interesting race.

Two days later we had another date with Louisville and, as was the case the previous season, I had a match-up problem with their backcourt. I had to guard 6'3" Jeff Hall and he finished with 22 points. Coach Denny Crum's 2-3 zone also limited openings for the drives Ernie Myers and I had used to defeat Duke. I was able to contribute 12 points and 4 assists.

We went to Atlanta to face Georgia Tech and emerged victors, 61–53. Nate McMillan played an especially courageous game. So ill with the flu that he had to take himself out of the game twice, Nate still was able to play 35 minutes and contributed 11 points. I had 6 points and 5 assists in 32 minutes.

Our next assignment was Wake Forest at Greensboro and my first real showdown with Mugsy Bogues. Bogues was superb, scoring 20 points with 10 assists and 4 steals, striking another blow for the little man. I stuck with him, nailing 9 of my 11 shots and scoring 18 points. Actually, Mugsy and I didn't truly square off because both teams employed zone defenses.

Unfortunately, Wake Forest could do little wrong and the Deacons routed us, 91–64. Their 48–26 rebounding edge and 65.6 shooting percentage in the first half told the story. "Wake was simply brilliant," Coach V said. "We played horribly, not to take anything away from Wake."

Now that Mugsy and I are both playing in the NBA, a lot of people ask me about him. I think that, realistically, he would not have been drafted in the first round if pro personnel people hadn't been convinced by me that a little man can play. That's no brag, just fact. Mugsy and I actually play with a very different sort of style. Although I'm technically a point guard, I'm more of a hybrid player who can shoot from the outside and push the ball upcourt. Mugsy is less of an offensive threat but on defense he flits around like a waterbug. You always have to worry about him when you have the ball.

The ACC race was the tightest in years. Only Virginia, with a 1–7 record, could be considered out of it. And even the Cavaliers were dangerous.

We helped ourselves considerably with a 69–57 victory over Clemson. I started, had 12 points and 8 assists and again amazed some people by pulling down 8 rebounds. Rebounding is like anything else: Determination is a key factor. Positioning is also important, as well as the element of surprise. A lot of times, a bigger player will be going after a rebound, see me, and figure he'll have no problem grabbing the ball. That hesitation is all I need to get an edge.

Next up was a nonconference game, one I'd been anxiously anticipating since the schedule was first announced. We were hosting Southern Methodist, from my hometown, Dallas, another Southwest Conference school that hadn't seen fit to seriously recruit me. The Mustangs were good, ranked fourth in the nation. Their center, Jon Koncak, eventually became my teammate with the Hawks.

We played one of our best games of the year in front of a national television audience, winning in overtime, 82–78. I started and had 17 points and 10 assists. Carl Wright, a guy I knew from Dallas, had 23 for the Mustangs, but I guarded him in the overtime and managed to hold him down. I canned a pair of free throws with six seconds left in overtime to ice the game after SMU had crept to within two.

We easily handled our next contest, against Maryland–Eastern Shore; but as always, we couldn't rest on our laurels. The North Carolina Tar Heels were on their way to our place, and an NC State win in this grudge match would considerably tighten the conference race. Media and fans could no longer say Carolina had our number.

The 85–76 victory was a sweet one for us, easily the biggest of my career at State. Now Georgia Tech was in the ACC lead by a half-game. We were 6–4, in a second-place tie with Carolina and Duke. Maryland was only a half-game behind us. And I was clearly starting to hit my stride as an offensive force. I shared scoring honors with Cozelle McQueen in the Carolina game, with 20 points and added 6 assists. I was able to really operate when Carolina switched to a man-to-man at the end of the game. With the floor spread I could work one-on-one, whirling to the hoop and wiggling inside for lay-ups over bigger men. "You have to hand this one today to Spud Webb and Cozelle McQueen and Terry Gannon," UNC coach Dean Smith told the reporters. "I haven't seen anyone play as well offensively as they did today."

We'd settled on a lineup of myself, Nate, Lo, Cozelle, and Ernie Myers with Terry Gannon and Pierre the first players off the bench. After the better part of two seasons, we were meshing as a unit. We weren't cocky but our confidence was growing. It was an exciting time for us.

We beat Duke, 70–66, at their crazy arena, with Lo scoring 25. I was right behind with 15 points, 5 assists, and 7 steals and made one of the game's biggest plays. Duke had evened the score at 66-all when I came up with a steal. I was fouled, and it was ruled to be intentional, much to the displeasure of the crowd. I hit both free throws with 49 seconds left, then made 1 of 2 with 12 seconds left, and it was over.

We edged Virginia, 57–55, then fell to Maryland, 71–70. So the regular-season ACC title boiled down to a rematch with Wake Forest. What a game it was: Senior Day, honoring our senior players, and the final college installment of my rivalry with Bogues. The crowd was really into it whenever we went at one another. The score was tied with less than 20 seconds to play and Mugsy was into his dribbling act, milking the clock before making his move to the basket. Somehow I was able to steal the ball, headed upcourt, was fouled, and hit the free throw to assure the victory. We finished with Carolina and Georgia Tech in a three-way tie for the ACC title.

No matter how we fared in the conference tournament in Atlanta, there was little chance that the NCAA committee could shut us out this time, not with our 19–8 record and share of the ACC crown.

We were seeded third in the tournament, drawing Clemson in the first round. We had a hard time shaking the Tigers but Gannon bottomed out a pair of jumpers to break a 59-all tie and we went on to a 70–63 triumph. Although I hit only 4 of 13 shots from the field, I converted 10 of 11 free throws and led the team with 18 points while playing all 40 minutes. We sank 20 of 24 from the foul line to ice the victory.

Round 3, State versus Carolina, awaited us the next afternoon. Kenny Smith and I battled the entire game and at the end he scored 5 points in the final 33 seconds to give the Tar Heels a 57–51 victory. I had 12 first-half points but finished with only 1 in the second half. We were dead tired after playing Clemson the previous night. The killer for us was that we made only 5 of 12 free throws. That could have been the product of fatigue.

We were disappointed, sure, but we also knew that Sunday would bring us the prize we were after, an NCAA bid. Sure enough, we got the word that we were being shipped out to Albuquerque, New Mexico, for the West Regional. Because of all the talented teams in the East, some of us had to be sent elsewhere. Albuquerque was a popular choice because it was there that the Wolfpack won the title in 1983. Our opponent, Nevada–Reno, was the Big Sky

Conference champion with a 21–9 record. Ironically, their nickname was the Wolf Pack. A team without a player taller than 6'7", Coach V said they were similar to Clemson and Wake Forest, a group of small but quick athletes. We won, 65–56, with Lo scoring 22 points and adding 23 rebounds. I had 11 points and 4 assists.

After the game I experienced a funny incident outside our locker room. When I tried to get in, a guard asked me, "Who are you?"

"I'm a player," I answered, pulling a pass out of my uniform pants as proof.

"You're a *player?*" the guy repeated doubtfully.

"Yep." I started down the steps to the locker room.

"Hey, you can't go down there," the guard yelled. "That's for the players."

I just shrugged and kept walking. I guess the guy hadn't had a chance to watch the game or that curious exchange wouldn't have been necessary.

Next we would face Texas–El Paso right in the Miners' backyard. "I'm more concerned about the hostile environment," Valvano said, speaking of the University of New Mexico's notorious arena, the Pit. "If there are 17,000 fans in there, 16,900 will probably be for UTEP. It's like an away game for us, so we'll have to draw on our road experience from the ACC."

We didn't know much about Texas–El Paso. They knew a lot about us, however, because of our TV exposure. In addition to the many nationally televised contests we appeared in, our games were on cable all the time. The Miners were concerned with me. "I'd almost rather play against bigger guards," Miners coach Don Haskins said. "We might have to get a fly swatter after Spud, I don't know."

The game was one I'll never forget. I scored a career-high 29 points—8 of 9 from the field, 13 of 17 from the line, and 7 assists—and we advanced in the tournament with an 86–73 decision. It was far and away the most thrilling offensive night I've ever had. I was in the zone. Everything I tossed up there went through the basket. It was almost an eerie feeling. Lo was also on fire, finishing with 30 points.

So we were moving on to the West Regional finals in Denver, catching Alabama in the opener. Alabama, 23–9, was approaching the game in Rodney Dangerfield fashion. "Nobody seems to realize we're here," 'Bama coach Wimp Sanderson said. "We don't get any respect." We could have made the same statement.

Our roll continued. We won, 61–55, to boost our record to 23–9. My roomie, Bennie Bolton, was the star. Bennie'd had an up-and-down career, spending a lot of time on Coach V's bad side. But he was great in the locker room, keeping everyone loose with his crazy antics. So we were all happy for him when he scored 8 first-half points, then nailed a pair of insurance free throws with 33 seconds to play to sew up the victory. Lo and I led the scoring with 14 apiece.

We were now breathing rarefied air, and I'm not talking about Denver's Mile High oxygen. We were in the West finals, one game away from the Final Four and a shot at a second national title in three years. Our opponent was St. John's in a rematch of the Holiday Festival finals.

The match-up was really special for Coach V, who had been friends with St. John's coach Lou Carnesecca. The first game Carnesecca ever coached was against Valvano's father, Rocco. When Jim Valvano coached at Iona, Carnesecca was always available to lend advice. Coach V couldn't wait for the game. "Hey, I'm pleasantly surprised to be here, considering the adversity we've had this season," Coach V said. We couldn't help but think what sort of team we'd have had if Chris Washburn hadn't gotten into trouble.

St. John's was ranked 2nd in the nation with a 30–3 record. We were 23–9, ranked 16th, not really considered in the class of the Redmen and their star-studded lineup. For all his coaching success, Carnesecca had never been in the Final Four and his players wanted to give him that present.

We led briefly in the early minutes but St. John's grabbed the advantage with about 12 minutes to go in the first half and never gave it up. We weren't dead, mind you. We were down by 7 early in the second half, then rallied to within a point with 11 minutes left in the game. But the Redmen shot nearly 80 percent from the free-throw line, 9 of 12 during one critical second-half stretch, for a 69–60 victory.

We had a few chances. I converted a three-point play to pull us to within 59–55 with 2:31 left, but after that we were never able to get closer than six. Had we ever gotten the lead, the plan was to spread the floor and let me operate. Coach V said he would have gone to the spread even if we were down by one or two points. But it never happened. I finished with 14 points and 9 assists and was named to the All-Tournament team along with Lo. I would have gladly turned in all my personal honors to win the game.

The season was a sweet ride. Only four schools reach the Final Four each March and St. John's had proved to be a better team. Personally, I had been tested, but I had proved that with faith in God and in your abilities you can achieve your goal. Perhaps, as Coach V says, I really am "The Little Engine That Could."

10

Working Toward the Dream

The end of a season is a strange time. We were all pretty low after the loss to St. John's because it left us one game short of making the NCAA Final Four, but there was also a sense of relief. The constant pressure from the media to repeat what the '83 Wolfpack team had done drove us all crazy, and now it was over. Looking back, I think we wanted it *too* much—making it to the Final Four was what everyone had on their minds, not the Redmen from St. John's. We just didn't concentrate, and even though we were in it all the way I think they deserved to win.

Back in the dorm the players relaxed and talked about the season, and I think everybody felt pretty good about it. We had gone 23–10 on the year, tied for first place in the ACC, and had a good showing in the Western Regionals. Now we could sit back and enjoy it for two or three weeks; by then, the media would be after us to predict what *next year's* team would be like.

That was not a main concern for us seniors. Our big topic was the draft: Who would make the NBA? Lorenzo was a shoo-in, and our center, Cozell McQueen, was mentioned a lot. But whenever a list of guards came out, saying which players the NBA scouts thought were pro material, my name was never there. Instead of worrying about it, I decided to concentrate on finishing school, since I had only 15 hours left for my degree.

I was on my way to sign up for summer school when the phone rang. That call would begin the craziest time of my life, and for the next six months my future would take more funny bounces than a lopsided basketball.

When the college season ended, I had asked Bill Blakeley, the one person who seemed to always believe in me, to represent me as my agent. Perhaps there was a wild chance that some NBA team might draft me. And now Bill was on the line.

"Spud, I think we've got some interest from the pros," he said.

Now I'm a confident guy, usually, but I've got to tell you that I couldn't quite believe what I'd just heard. I tried to come up with an articulate, self-possessed reply to such phenomenal news.

"Huh?"

What I didn't know was that Bill had been out pestering scouts and coaches with various teams on my behalf, telling them that I was the greatest point guard since Oscar Robertson—notwithstanding the fact that Oscar was 6'5". Anyway, Bill told me to come to Dallas as soon as possible to go over my plans before the NBA draft in mid-June.

I met Bill at his offices near downtown Dallas, where Talent Sports International is headquartered. TSI was founded by a super-sharp Dallas attorney named Craig Massey. Massey hired Bill's son, Robin Blakeley, away from ProServ sports management in New York, and the two of them built up the company from the events/marketing side, while Bill, the crusty old basketball coach, handles all the recruiting. I knew I was in good hands from the beginning, because the Blakeleys had been loyal to me for a long time, and all three men had strong Christian backgrounds. That was very important to me, because as an athlete you're always hearing horror stories about bad agents misrepresenting themselves or their clients. I knew right away that the whole TSI group was impeccably honest.

And pretty aggressive, too, because the minute I walked in the door they told me they already had a deal in the works with the Pony shoes people, who had followed my career at NC State. Now remember, I was still a tremendous longshot to even get *drafted,* much less a star big enough to get a shoe deal. But the Blakeleys were incredibly positive, and I started getting a little excited myself.

We decided I should get as much exposure and playing time as possible in the next two months, so I played in the annual Portsmouth Tournament, a game for college seniors held in Norfolk, Virginia. Postseason games like this can be kind of silly because everyone hogs the ball, trying to show all the pro scouts in the stands what scoring machines they are. After the game, a lot of scouts seek out certain players to discuss the player's plans and to see how the player carries himself. I walked slowly off the court— *very* slowly—but no coaches came up to talk to me and I couldn't help but wonder if there would ever be any interest at all in me.

The next week I got another call from Bill, this one to tell me that I was going to play pro basketball after all . . . sort of. A new semipro summer league known as the United States Basketball League was opening up and the coach of the Rhode Island Gulls wanted me to play for them. Blakeley was cautiously enthusiastic.

"Spud, the league is getting some good talent, and I think at this point it might be a good move," he said.

"They say they'll pay you a thousand a week plus a three-thousand-dollar signing bonus if you start within two weeks. Heck, you could even pay off that fancy yellow Corvette of yours."

I love Dallas and the few weeks I spent with my family after the Portsmouth game were great, but I was ready to leave. Walking around my old neighborhood, I got depressed seeing how many of my friends were wasting their lives. They had dropped out of school to take nowhere jobs and a lot of them hadn't even tried to get jobs. They just sat around the house, talking about what they *could* have done if only they'd had some breaks. This infuriated me. Sure, some of the guys had legitimate personal problems or obstacles, but a lot of folks had all sorts of things going for them—a lot more size and talent than I had, for instance—but they didn't use them. It makes you mad when you see that. Mookie and I used to call them "dream chasers." In the afternoon pickup games at the rec center these guys would always be saying stuff like, "Check out my Magic Johnson special, man," and then they'd try some fancy move to the hole, probably missing the basket completely. They were always criticizing the lesser NBA players, saying, "That so-and-so, he's a joke. When we played his team my senior year at The Hutch, I cleaned his clock and sent him home cryin', man!" Mookie and I would roll our eyes and laugh. But it really isn't funny. It's sad to see how many fine young athletes never stretch far enough to reach their true potential.

Newport, Rhode Island, is the farthest thing from Wilmer Hutchins I've ever seen. You don't see many brothers there. It seems to be a resort area for white folk—make that *old* white folk—who all live in big houses and have boats down at the harbor. The one thing they do have is lots of fresh shrimp, which is my favorite food. No jokes, please.

When the blue bloods in the area weren't sunning on their yachts or redecorating their mansions, they proved to be a lively crowd of basketball fans, which was good for our new team. We had two big stars, John "Hot Rod" Williams, from Tulane, and Manute Bol, the 7'7" African who had played one season at the University of Bridgeport in Connecticut. Our coach was Kevin Stacum, a former Boston Celtics star who turned out to be a great guy. In fact, he was too nice to be a coach. But Kevin helped us a lot with our games, working on the important fundamentals he'd learned from Red Auerbach during those Celtic glory years.

The USBL had only seven teams, each playing a 25-game schedule. The games were wide open and fun to play. They could be pretty rough sometimes, and the lack of finesse reminded me of some of our battles at Highland Hills rec center back in Dallas. Nothing too fancy, just lace 'em up and get at it.

During our off hours, the players gathered at a bar Kevin owned down by the wharf, appropriately named "The Dockside Saloon." I never drink alcohol, but since it was Kevin's place (and he was the coach!) I went down there too and traded stories with my teammates. We all agreed on two things: Each of us wanted to play in the NBA, and we all thought Rhode Island was the most boring place in the world.

When we weren't down at the Dockside, we were in our apartments or, if were were on the road, in our hotel rooms. Basketball players spend *lots* of time in hotel rooms. Funny as it may seem, the guy I became best friends with during these long stretches of time was Manute.

The press liked to make a big deal about the difference

in our height, but I think that brought us closer together. Our common ground was a desire to make people stop thinking about how tall we were (or weren't), and start seeing us as all-around basketball players. We didn't have much luck in those days. Whenever people saw us standing together they wanted to take our picture. Photographers constantly asked us to stand side by side while somebody squeezed in between us like we were bookends or something. At first it was funny, but it got old real fast. We both began to hate the way people treated us like freaks, and we spent more and more time in our rooms.

Manute is a funny guy. He loves to joke, and he cusses his head off although I don't think he knows what all the words mean. He used to call me "Big Man," and he just called himself "Bol." He'd say stuff like, "Bol is hungry. Hey, Big Man, take Bol out and buy him dinner since you are rich American." That's something you rarely wanted to do, because the guy can eat like a horse. Manute is a Dinka tribesman from the Sudan, and over there they must have superfast metabolisms. If you or I ate as much as Manute, we'd look like Refrigerator Perry of the Chicago Bears, but Manute burns it right up. When we were playing for the Gulls, he weighed only 180 pounds.

I could listen for hours to Manute, which is good because he talks a lot. In our hotel room, me in a chair and Manute sprawled diagonally across a king-sized bed, he'd tell stories about being a farmer and rancher in the Sudan, about how he walked for miles through the desert and killed lions with a wooden spear. During a game, when one of the opposing team's centers would rough Manute up he'd say, "I wish I had my spear tonight. I'd keep it in my sock, and when that fat bastard try to chop at me with those elbows, Bol show him a thing or two." Manute was often homesick, especially since his father (who was 7'8", by the way) had died less than a year before. Manute hoped he would make lots of money playing basketball so he could afford to visit his mother and sister in Africa. As it was, the $1,000 he got each week for playing in Rhode Island was about 150 times what the average Sudanese brought home per week.

Manute probably has every penny he ever made because you hardly ever see the guy spend money. And when he does, he always pays in cash, saying he doesn't understand the American obsession with credit cards.

"I leave home without it," he says. "American people don't want to pay for what they buy. Bol can pay."

Another funny thing about Manute. Even though he had no car, and lived in the same student apartment complex that I did, 20 minutes from downtown, he still managed to get around without hitching a ride from any of the players. He was everywhere. You go to practice, he's already there. You go to the game, he's already there. So you ask him how he got there and he says something like, "Hey, Big Man, I get here. Telephone, don't walk." Nobody ever knew what the last part meant, but Manute has a way of speaking that is all his own.

The team was playing about .500 and Hot Rod was the leading scorer. He was averaging 23 points a game and I was next with 20, which made me feel good even though I'm not real big on statistics. It was a tough time for Hot Rod, however, because he had been indicted in a point-shaving scandal—I think the legal term is "sports bribery" —during his last year at Tulane, and he had to keep leaving the team to make court appearances. He told us he was innocent, and later he was cleared of all charges. We were all happy for him, because Hot Rod has had a tough life: His mom died when he was a baby, and his dad abandoned him soon after that. He was raised by neighbors in a cramped, dilapidated house trailer in Sorrento, Louisiana. Because he was a fantastic basketball player in high school, he got a scholarship to Tulane, a very tough school academically, even though he didn't exactly shine on his SATs. Because he was such a star, nobody ever pressured him to learn at school, and he was shy and quiet. He played great for Tulane, becoming Metro Conference Player of the Year when he was a junior, but then came his arrest with three other players his senior year for point-shaving. The jury said there simply wasn't enough evidence and they acquitted him.

Nobody ever offered me any big sums of cash for anything in college, but when you hear how poor some of these guys were, and how uneducated they were in the policies and politics of big-time college athletics, you understand why they take what is offered to them. I'm not saying it's right, but I don't think the people who judge them have a realistic idea of what pressures a lot of these guys are under—from their families, their friends, and even the alumni. In any case, my heart went out to Hot Rod, and I was reminded of how lucky I've been to have a loving family around me to help make intelligent decisions.

Hot Rod soon left Rhode Island to join the Cleveland Cavaliers and he became a star in the NBA. *A star in the NBA.* That seemed so far away even then. Coach Stacum used to give us tips in practice on how to try out for a pro team. He taught us different kinds of head fakes, how to use picks to get open, and how to shoot off the pick as soon as you get the ball. In my heart I felt I could make it in the NBA, and play with the best of the best. But would I get the chance?

June 14, 1985. I came home from practice and the phone was ringing. It was my sister Stephanie, calling from Dallas.

"Spud! You've been drafted, baby! It just came over the TV!"

"Who was it, Steph?" I asked.

"Detroit! Let's see, they picked you in the fourth round!"

Stephanie, my old one-on-one partner growing up, sounded as excited as I was. My sister Renee told me that Stephanie had gotten into a shouting match and almost into a fight on the bus recently because some guy told her I wasn't NBA material. Those are fighting words to Steph, who is fiercely loyal to me. Now she would have the last laugh.

About five minutes later, I heard the unmistakable sound of Manute's size-15½ feet clomping up to my apartment door.

"Open up, Big Man! Bol has been drafted to Washington. Bol will play basketball for your president!"

We were both ecstatic and kept laughing about what our futures might be. Manute, who as I said is the most tight-fisted guy you ever saw, wanted to know if I could get him a good deal on a car in Detroit.

"But Manute, I haven't made the team yet," I said.

"You will, Big Man," he replied, his white teeth flashing behind his shining, coal-black face. "You are a hard worker. I am too. People say you are too small, that I am too skinny to play NBA. We will show then. We will work hard and become big stars."

I had to leave Rhode Island right away for rookie camp in Detroit. Honestly, I was so excited just to be *drafted* that I didn't get nervous about the tryout. Sure, I knew in the NBA fourth-round draft picks don't usually stay around to make the team. But on the plane flight up all I wondered about was what it would be like playing against the greatest players in the world. I thought about stepping on the court with Dr. J to play the Sixers: How would it feel? How good were these guys compared to what I had faced in college? These questions would be answered soon enough.

I did decide one thing: I wasn't going to be intimidated. I would go out on that court and play my best. *If it happens, it happens.* If I got cut, I wasn't going to go jump off some bridge. I was in fine shape, and I hoped if I tried my hardest, good things would happen.

Miracles were what needed to happen. There were 15 rookies in camp and we learned right away that only one point-guard position was open. The starting job was filled by a guy named Isiah Thomas, an All-Star MVP and one of the top guards ever to play in the NBA. And at the shooting spot, the Pistons had used their number-one pick to get Joe Dumars, the ninth leading scorer in NCAA history, from McNeese State in Louisiana. Since Dumars had Bill Blakeley as his agent, I knew how good Joe was and we became great friends. Joe is kind of quiet like I am, but watch out for him; he's strong, smart, and quick, and even though people like Adrian Dantley, Isiah, and Vinnie Johnson get all the publicity as the hot shooters, time will tell that Joe is the best pure shooter on that team. He'll be in the league a long time.

We played at a college in Detroit for two days and then in Chicago for three days. It was one of the toughest workouts I've ever experienced. You play for four hours in the morning, go home and sleep because you're exhausted, then come back and play again that night. It's nonstop, full-tilt action and everyone is trying to get the coaches to notice them. After it's all over, you go home and wait for a phone call.

What I got was a letter. A "Dear Spud" letter. Detroit had enough guards, it said, and they wished me well "in future endeavors." Before I could guess what those might be, Bill Blakeley called to say that the Harlem Globetrotters were interested. "They think you would fit perfectly into their show," he said. I wasn't so sure.

On the positive side, playing with the Globetrotters would mean traveling all over the world, being an ambassador of sorts, and that appealed to me. So did the fact that so much of the Globetrotter show is geared to kids, and I love working with kids. But for all their undeniable natural talent, the Globetrotters are about showmanship, not competitive basketball skill. Playing, or should I say, performing with them would lose a lot for me because I love the competitive nature of the sport. Also, I figured that the 'Trotters would put together skits making fun of my height, and that was the last thing I wanted to do.

Finally, I decided not to do it. I think it goes back to what I said about being with Manute; you want people to respect you and enjoy your ability, not laugh at your size or some oddball thing you do. Bill and Robin both applauded my decision, saying that I still had a chance with Atlanta, where assistant coach Brendan Suhr said he thought I had a real chance.

My chances got better when the Hawks' starting point guard, Glenn "Doc" Rivers, fractured his wrist. Atlanta's head coach Mike Fratello told his assistant coaches they needed someone quick who could push the ball upcourt during training camp until Doc's wrist healed. Summoning all his courage, Brendan suggested the name Spud Webb. He knew Fratello couldn't make too much out of my height because Mike is only 5'7" himself, when he's wearing his Gucci loafers. Fratello looked at my tape and told Brendan to call my agent and arrange to get me in camp ASAP.

A second chance! The news gave me a real lift. I always told myself that I would be happy just to be drafted, but after I got cut from Detroit I knew that wasn't the case. Before the Hawks called I even thought about looking for a coaching job, but that was simply a backup plan. What I had wanted from the beginning was to play basketball in the NBA. I wanted it with all my heart and soul, and now I had another chance to get it.

When a 5'7", 130-pound man walks into an NBA training camp, people do a doubletake. I could see the smiles on the players' faces, and the looks of disbelief worn by the team's management. So much for introductions. Now it was time to play basketball.

The Hawks had a very young team and were coming off a disappointing 34–48 year. The team had no real identity; rather, it revolved around the amazing talents of Dominique Wilkins, who *was* the franchise. Dominique is truly remarkable, but no one player can carry an NBA team to a championship, and the Hawks' braintrust— Michael Gearon, the team chairman; Stan Kasten, the president and general manager; and head coach Fratello— was constantly meeting, discussing trades, drafts, and realignment of players to somehow come up with a combination of talent that might restore the Hawks to their glory of 1979–80, when they went 50–32 under coach Hubie Brown and won the Central Division. It was the only 50-win season in Atlanta's history, and the Hawks fans wanted some of that old excitement.

I wanted to help bring that excitement back, but first I had to convince a very skeptical audience. While I practiced, the media was scrutinizing every move. Jeff Denberg, basketball beat writer for the *Atlanta Journal-Constitution,* was intrigued by me, but he decided to call up the head of NBA scouting, Marty Blake, and get some real scoop.

"Hey Marty, this is Jeff Denberg in Atlanta. I'm calling about this kid Spud Webb. Is he for real, or what?"

"Well, Jeff, when I heard Detroit had cut him, I figured he got squashed or something, but then you look at the guards they already had in camp, and he never really had a chance," said Blake. "Now, Atlanta is a different story. They've got the youth to be a good running team, and Spud is greased lightning."

"Yeah, but can he play defense?" asked Denberg, a tough-talking New Yorker who doesn't beat around the bush. "I mean, I'm looking at this kid, and he's so damn spindly and small, I'm wondering if he needs a helmet and some shoulder pads."

Blake laughed. "No question Spud could use 'em, but don't be fooled. Too many times when we rate players, we do it negatively. You have to look at what Spud *can* do for you. He's an attack weapon, changing tempo and putting pressure on the other team. Sure he's got some liabilities, but who doesn't?"

"Well, all I know is that Kasten thinks the kid is a joke. Some of the writers were asking him about Spud today and he said Spud was 'just somebody to push the ball upcourt.' I think Stan's afraid people will laugh if he puts the kid in a uniform."

"He may not have to worry about that," replied Blake. "You guys play the Knicks on Sunday. That means Spud will have to survive Patrick Ewing."

I had to survive the Hawks' training camp first, and I soon found out that was no small task. On Wednesday afternoon before we were to go to New York, my pro career came to an abrupt halt.

It was another hard scrimmage, with rookies giving their all for a place on the team roster. I was guarding a fellow rookie, Cedric Toney, who was racing down the floor. Cedric got slightly ahead of me, and as his back turned, I reached around to try to steal the ball. He caught my theft attempt out of the corner of his eye, and threw a vicious elbow my way to discourage me. I should have taken the hint. Cedric is very strong, and the elbow hit me full force right in the face. I felt I had been hit in the nose by a sledgehammer. Blood poured out all over my face and neck, and there was so much I couldn't see. My teeth had clenched on impact, cutting my top lip almost clean through in the process.

I crumpled to the ground. Blood was puddling on the dusty gym floor, as trainer Joe O'Toole came scrambling over to assess the damage. He signaled to an assistant, they helped me to a van and we sped to the hospital. In the emergency room, the doctors cleaned off the blood and began stitching the lip back on. I remember hearing one of the doctors tell a nurse, "Bring a lot of thread. This one is messy."

In all, it took 44 stitches, on both the inside and outside of my mouth, to sew the lip back together. Furthermore, my head had swollen half again as big from the force of the blow, as if it were one huge bruise. When I left the hospital, my head was so bandaged up I couldn't talk and could barely see. The doctors had said the swelling would take three days to go down, and that I shouldn't practice for at least two weeks.

Two weeks! It couldn't be. Lying in bed with my head throbbing, I sorted out my options. If I didn't practice in the next two days, the coaches probably wouldn't let me play any more preseason games. If I didn't play any more preseason, then my chances of staying on the team were slim indeed. But what about the warnings from the doctors —should I play even if I could? I wanted to talk to a friend about it, but I was too bandaged up to speak.

On Friday morning I sat in the locker room alone, feeling discouraged and in pain. My teammates were outside practicing, and my dream was slowly slipping away. I remembered how I felt as a teenager, after not making the high school varsity team. I was sad and angry then, too, but my sisters reminded me, "No one in this family is a quitter. Go out and make us proud." I bowed my head to pray.

"Lord, this is a once-in-a-lifetime chance. If I don't play, they'll cut me. I can't talk, so I have to go out there and prove what I can do with the ability you gave me. Help me put aside the pain and concentrate on the game. I am weak, Lord, but you are strong, and now more than ever, I need your strength on my side. Amen."

I put on my practice gear and reported to Fratello, bandages and all. "I'm ready to play, coach."

I started the game against the Knicks, and played on sheer instinct. Because of the stitches, everyone assumed that I would stay way outside away from any danger, and do little more than pass the ball around. As Jeff Denberg later wrote, that wasn't the case.

"On the first play, a fast break opportunity opened up. Spud took the outlet pass from Kevin Willis, and charged upcourt. He looked toward Dominique, and the Knicks defense shifted ever so slightly in that direction. Spud juked his man with a lightning quick stutter step, then headed into the lane where Ewing was standing like the Sears Tower. Spud head-faked him once, then took flight from just inside the free throw line as blue jerseys converged to envelop him. Suddenly Spud reappeared, soaring over the disbelieving Ewing, and the little man dished the ball to Dominique, who jammed it through the hoop. It was dynamic. The dunk sent the crowd into a frenzy and the Hawks players were leading the cheers. This scrawny kid, who's supposed to be in the hospital, had just made a great play over the league's top prospect. Spud Webb has more than great basketball talent; he has courage and toughness, and he deserves to play in the NBA."

I felt good that we had won the game and knew I had played well. Coming off the floor, I was surprised to find how good I felt. There was some throbbing, but the joy of playing well more than compensated for it. We can do so much more than we think we can if we listen to our minds, not our bodies. Still, I had new respect for professional athletes who play with pain.

The other players made the moment sweet. Crowding around me, they offered their congratulations and more importantly, their support. Dominique put his arm around me and announced, "This is my main man, you all. I don't want anybody messing with him." Everyone laughed, but his message was clear: Dominique wanted me on the team, and everybody heard it. (I think it's because I pass him the ball so much.) More encouragement came from Cliff Levingston and Tree Rollins, the old pro who had seen many rookies come and go. "You proved yourself out there, Little Man. You made me a believer."

The most important words came later from coach Fratello.

"Spud, because I can look you in the eye, no one appreciates more than I what you've accomplished in getting here," he said. "You probably know that just about everyone was skeptical about your chances to make this team, but I want you to know right now that I think you are a young man with great talent and promise, and I'm proud to offer you a place on this team. Welcome to the NBA."

There are moments in your life when you feel so good, so deeply happy, that you simply can't describe it. It's a feeling that goes beyong jumping and hollering, beyond slapping backs and shaking hands. It's a feeling way down inside you that wells up into your heart and says, "You did it." I guess the best description I've heard is from mountain climbers, who, after a grueling, painful climb to the top, stand quietly at the summit and consider their achievement.

For the last nine years of my life, I had been utterly dedicated to one goal, which everyone told me was impossible. Now, standing here knowing that I had done it, I felt so proud of what I had done. All those things my parents told me, about hard work, trusting God, and believing in yourself *really were true!*

Nobody waltzes into the NBA. You can only get there with long, hard work, no matter how talented you are. But being the shortest player ever to get in, I agreed with that old slogan, "The roughest road is the best way of getting there." No matter what happened to me from here on, for the rest of my life, I would always know that I had accomplished something unique. And when people called me a shrimp or a square, or questioned my devotion to what I love, I needed only to look back at the path I had traveled, with all of its rocks and roadblocks, and remember that I rose above those obstacles and achieved a lifelong dream. In less than a month, I would step out onto a basketball court wearing an Atlanta Hawks uniform. Outside, perhaps, all people would see was a young black man with his game face on, a pro basketball player only 5'6" tall. That wasn't going to matter. Inside, I was already flying high.

A Giant Leap of Faith

One lesson you learn quickly in the NBA: Nobody gives a rookie *anything*. You've got to prove what you can do, and show how tough you are right from the beginning, or the veterans will eat you alive. Not to mention the coaches. At this level, everybody already knows you can play, and play well. The big question is, can you *win?*

Winning is the greatest feeling in the world, and no one has to sell me on it. But I knew from the first day that my challenge was to earn respect, to prove myself to the NBA players and coaches the same way I had been proving myself over and over all my life.

I had signed a one-year contract with the Hawks for $70,000, which is the league minimum salary. Stan Kasten said the team wasn't about to offer a penny more, which my agent told me was Kasten's way of saying, "No way the kid will last." In fact, the Hawks made it clear that they could release me anytime before December 10 without having to fulfill the whole contract, so I knew I'd better start contributing right away. That might have made another player nervous, but I've lived with that kind of doubt since junior high school.

Before I played my first NBA game, I had already made my first TV commercial. It was a 30-second spot for Pony shoes, featuring me and Orlando Woolridge of the Chicago Bulls. In the commercial, Orlando (who's a high-flying 6'9" forward) goes in for an awesome dunk, then flips the ball to this short kid who's supposed to follow suit. The producer's problem was, "Where in the world are we going to find a really small kid who can take only one step toward the basket, go straight up and dunk?"

Well, the kid is in the book. Look under "Spud."

The Pony people originally offered me $5,000, which I was perfectly willing to take since I hadn't yet had my tryout with the Hawks and was facing a very uncertain future. But my agent Robin Blakeley told them, "No way. There are only three or four guys in the whole country who can pull off what you want with the right style, and since Spud is going to be a huge star [Robin has always been very optimistic], we've got to have a lot more money." They were down to the deadline in shooting the commercial, so Pony gave in and gave me $20,000. I was one happy boy, let me tell you, and that began a long and very friendly relationship with Pony shoes.

Coming up to the first game of the season, the Hawks had still not signed veteran guards Eddie Johnson or Mike Glenn, and Glenn Rivers still had a fractured wrist. That left the point guard spot up for grabs, and the day before the game Coach Fratello told me that I would be starting.

Starting!

Two months ago I was sitting at home, having been cut from the Pistons, with no prospect for *any* job, much less a chance to play in the NBA. Now suddenly here I was, putting on an Atlanta Hawks uniform, about to go out and play with people like Dominique Wilkins and Tree Rollins.

Game time was an hour away, and out on the court, members of the Washington Bullets—our first opponent —were warming up. Kevin Willis and Cliff Levingston, always the first Hawks out of the locker room for warm-ups, were shooting baskets. "Helps get the butterflies out," Cliff grinned, knowing how nervous I must be. Around us was the massive Omni complex, which is headquarters for Ted Turner's sports/media conglomerate. Ted would soon be strolling in for the game, one of 10,129 people who would witness my very first pro basketball performance.

I was excited to learn that the Hawks hold a chapel before every home game, and about half the players attend. I was there on bended knee, trying to get calm and asking the Lord to be with me on this important night. Mostly my prayer was one of thanks, that He had given me a healthy body and mind, and now this incredible opportunity to used them playing the game I love. By the time I left the chapel service, a sense of peace had come over me. When I walked out onto that court, I knew I was not alone.

As we lined up for the tip-off, Dominique gave me a wink. He had "adopted" me from the first day, and already we had become good friends. Everyone knows what an unbelievable athlete he is, but he is also a very kind and gentle guy. Our new offense had been geared to run, and nobody flies downcourt on the wing better than Dominique. In practice we worked on all sorts of alley-oop plays, where I throw the ball way up above the basket, and Dominique swoops in from the baseline, grabs the ball at the top of the leap, and jams it home with a dunk. With his phenomenal leaping ability, Dominique can grab even the lousiest pass and score with it, making both of you look good.

That was part of our strategy. We had to do something creative, because the Bullets were playing with my old USBL buddy, Manute Bol. Before the game, Manute and I met at midcourt and shook hands, his 7'7" frame looming over me, at 5'7" in my sneakers. "Well, Little Man, we are here!" he said with excitement in his eyes. "And listen. Don't you try none of that dunking, because Bol will block your shot!"

Bol wasn't lying. He swatted away several shots that night, and went on to lead the league that year with 397 blocked shots. I was proud of him, but I still wanted to score on him.

Before I could score on anybody, though, I had to get past a guy named Gus Williams. That's right, the "Wizard," the guy who I had imitated a thousand times growing up, was guarding me down the floor, using his famous stutter-step to freeze me while he zipped passes to his teammates. Being so close, I found myself almost being a spectator. Here's one time when having a good field of vision is not an advantage. I've heard a lot of NBA players say they've experienced the same thing from time to time; there you are, playing against an extraordinary athlete who can do amazing things, and you find yourself temporarily suspended in time, unable to stop watching them.

We were down at the half, and in the locker room our trainer Joe O'Toole attended to various medical complaints while the coaches worked busily at the blackboard. Coach Reed was exhorting Tree to muscle Manute, who was clearly not strong enough to box the 245-pound Tree out of the lane. I was getting pointers from Glenn Rivers (who we all call "Doc"), the man whose place I was taking. Doc is two years ahead of me and a real competitor; he wanted to share his tips on going against the Bullets, in the hope we could turn things around and win our opener.

Unfortunately, we lost 100–91, even though I had a

strong game. I hit 5 out of 7 shots and both free throws, finishing with 12 points and 10 assists. Playing well in that first game gave me great satisfaction—I felt a sense of belonging and warmth like I had never known before. And now, for the rest of my life, I could say that I had played in the NBA. Someone hollered, "Hey, Spud! You just made the record books, man!" Because of my height, I would go down as the shortest player ever. Nothing could have meant less to me. This feeling of having succeeded was what mattered; it was worth more than any statistic or award I could ever receive. I had accomplished a goal that everyone said was impossible.

In a crazy sort of way, so had my buddy Manute. Here he was, this gangly, scared kid from Africa (nobody knows how old he really is, because in the Sudan they don't keep track of that stuff) who wanted to see America. He spoke almost no English at all, and was so tall and skinny that he literally did not fit in anywhere, yet he stood out everywhere. He was just as committed to success, hoping to make some money for himself and his family. In making the Bullets, he had experienced a similar thrill to mine, and his team had won. He too had just set a record—for being the tallest player ever in the NBA. I was happy for Manute, but disappointed that I could not quarterback my team to a win my first time out. Manute must have known how I felt, because he came straight over to me after the game and told me how well I played.

"You damn good, Little Man," he said. "Hardly miss a single shot."

"Thanks, Manute," I replied. "But we probably would have won if you hadn't blocked all our shots."

"That is Bol's purpose," he grinned. "You run and shoot. Bol stands and blocks!"

It was a great moment for us both, standing there on the Omni floor having played a game we dreamed about.

Soon, just about everyone had gone to the locker room, and Manute reached out with his big long fingers and took my hand. Together we walked off the court, two great friends who happened to be the bookends of professional basketball.

One week and a couple of games later, we played Boston in the famed Boston Garden. Talk about a shock. For all its great history and nostalgic feel, that place is a dump. It's either way too hot or freezing cold, the locker rooms leak, and the parquet floor you hear so much about is cracked, lumpy and uneven. But it's still the greatest place in the world to play.

I get into all that basketball history stuff. Looking up at the ceiling full of "World Champions" banners, you think back to all the great players who carved out careers in that broken-down gym: Bob Cousy, Bill Russell, John Havlicek, Paul Silas, Don Chaney. You think of the *pride* those guys had in the game, playing unselfishly, as a team. I wish we had more of that in modern basketball. I've noticed our Atlanta fans are becoming more like the Boston fans —they really know their basketball, and they cheer you for a great play even if you're on the opposing team. It doesn't hurt that Boston still has great teams year after year, and here I was, a rookie with only three pro games under my belt, about to go against Dennis Johnson, Larry Bird, Kevin McHale, and the rest of the Celtics, who just happened to be the reigning world champions.

I had a good game against Boston, but we lost again, 109–105. It was a wild game, and I don't think McHale and Robert Parrish knew what to make of me. Starting from the top of the key, I would furiously drive the lane and go up for the shot. Then, just as the two big men converged on me, I dished off to Dominique or Kevin Willis for the easy jam. That play was soon to become a trademark for me during my young NBA career. As for the loss, well, Boston lost only *one* game at home all season, and that was when two of their men were out sick.

The next night we were back in Atlanta, and a lifelong dream of mine was about to be fulfilled. We were matched against the Philadelphia 76ers, and that meant I'd be playing on the same court with the modern-time legend of basketball, Dr. J.

The game was fun and frantic, seesawing back and forth until the very end, when we managed to send it into overtime. The only problem was, three of our veterans fouled out, and it was left to us rookies to take charge in the stretch. In fact, my two roommates—Lorenzo Charles and John Battle—and I were fighting it out along with Jon Koncak, a seven-footer from SMU, and one "old" guy, one-year vet Kevin Willis. It was fantastic! Playing against Julius Erving, and alongside my NC State buddy Lo. The final score, you ask? 114–113, good guys! The Omni was blasting off, feeling the enthusiasm of these rookies who put on a show in overtime.

It was only our second win of the season, and we enjoyed every bit of it. Everyone went out after the game, and I don't think we got home until about 3 A.M. The phone rang all night and people kept coming over. We all got lots of ribbing at our next practice, and Tree announced, "Well, now that you babies have won one whole game, I guess it's time we rearranged the starting lineup." Everyone laughed knowingly. We still had a lot to learn.

Especially me, I'm afraid, because suddenly I was playing terribly. The team was on a western road trip, and I started turning the ball over a lot, making some sloppy passes and misreading some defenses. My own defense was poor, and early on in one game Coach Fratello benched me. I hated that! Nobody's playing ever got better from sitting on a bench, but that's how coaches react with rookies. Forget "playing through" your slumps—you just better snap out of them. So then I started pressing everything when I played, and the pressure I put on myself just made everything worse. In seven games I took just eight shots, making only one. I tried to go to the hole, and suddenly everything was shut off.

Tree was a real friend. "You've got rookie-itis," he said to me. "Just slow down, play your game. The season is one hundred games, man, and nobody can be a star every time. You'll bounce back. Use your mental toughness, 'cause in the NBA you need it every night."

I've always thought I was mentally tough, but there are so many distractions in pro sports that you have to block out everything when you walk out onto the court. I was getting a lot of media attention at the time because of my height, and in every town we played in the local papers wanted an interview: The same questions, over and over. . . . That repetition gets extremely dull after a while, and if you're 5'7" the short jokes become unbearably predictable.

One media spot I turned down was *Late Night with David Letterman*. Actually, I love Letterman, but he had been doing a series of shows with some odd sports figures like baseball pitcher Terry Forster (who he called "a fat tub of goo") and Refrigerator Perry; Bill Needle, the Hawks' p.r. director, thought the Letterman people were looking more for freak show material than a real interview. Fratello heard I had been asked to do the show, and in the Phoenix airport that day he decided to have some fun with me.

"Hey, Spud," he said as we waited for our plane, "don't I include you guys in everything—have you over to the house for dinner, and for a Christmas party?"

"Yeah, Coach," I replied.

"Then how come I hear you're going on the David Letterman show and you don't tell these people that you have to bring your coach along?"

"I did," I answered. "That's why I'm not doing the Letterman show."

Over the next few games I had a few good moments—like a blocked shot against Golden State's Terry Teagle which I swatted away, caught up with, and then dunked at the other end of the court while the Oakland crowd went crazy—but mostly I was in a shell of fear and uncertainty. I knew Stan Kasten wanted me cut and Ray Williams (brother of Gus) kept on the team. The December 10 cut deadline was approaching, and it seemed a lot more sensible to Kasten to keep a guy like Ray, who had plenty of court savvy and eight high-scoring seasons under his belt in the NBA. Still, Ray was out of shape from not having played lately, and he, too, was in a shooting slump. It was a tough call, and the decision was Coach Fratello's to make.

On December 4, we played Portland at the Omni and Doc Rivers was back in the lineup. Talk about comebacks. Doc was a machine, scoring 16 points, handing out 10 assists, and getting a career-high 8 steals in leading us to a 109–98 victory. Watching him play, I gained new respect for his abilities, and saw how much he had missed the action as the Hawks' starting point guard. It's a good thing I was comfortable with my role of coming off the bench, because Doc was sending a clear message: He was here to play.

But was I? The night before the Milwaukee game, sportswriter Jeff Denberg called Coach Fratello at home. He had the same question in mind I had.

"Mike, I sense you're under a lot of pressure to get rid

of Spud—" Denberg probed. But before he could finish his sentence, Fratello shot back.

"I don't give a damn what Stan says or anybody else," he cried. "Spud stays! And you can put that in the bank!"

The next morning, Ray Williams was waived.

Christmas was approaching, and we had one last game to play, against the Houston Rockets. The first half of the season had been up and down—we were winning at home (11–4) but getting pounding on the road (2–10). It just goes to show what a huge advantage the home court is in pro basketball; much more, I think, than in football or baseball. A court is a very personal space, and you begin to learn certain spots on the floor where you like to shoot. You get comfortable with the lighting, how the ball plays off the rim (some rims are "hard" while others are "soft," meaning they have more give when the ball hits), and because you know the stripes and paint on your own floor, you always know where you are in relation to the basket. That is a definite advantage, because you can have your back to the basket, yet still be able to spin and shoot in the blink of an eye. On an opponent's court, it takes that tiny split second to look up and see where you are, and that can be the difference between an open shot or having a defender in your face.

Tonight we were on our home court. And we needed a little Christmas.

The Rockets were red-hot, coming off a 48-win season and sporting their "Twin Towers," 7'4" Ralph Sampson and 6'11" Akeem "The Dream" Olajuwon. Our team was still in a slump of sorts, not even playing .500 ball.

The pace was fast from the beginning—our running game against their running game, with the big men for both teams battling like Spartan warriors underneath. There were some serious elbows flying, and even yours truly was a little skittish about driving into the middle of that action, especially since I'm about elbow-high to most seven-footers. But since the game was a footrace, Coach Fratello had me in there for almost 20 minutes.

I should mention that while the big guys were dominating the game, my adopted big brother, 'Nique Wilkins, was lighting up the scoreboard like a pinball machine. And with less than a minute to go, he hit a levitation jumper with three, count 'em, three guys on him to send the game into overtime. The small holiday crowd of 8,600 at the Omni was getting its money's worth. In the overtime, Houston scored with only 11 seconds left to go, and so they were up, 122–120.

Crowds love this and coaches dread it—do you go for the easier two-point basket and tie, or do you take the very chancy three-point shot for a win? Mike Fratello had an out; he could give the ball to Dominique and let *him* decide.

The play was set to go inside, and Dominique took the inbounds pass looking for an opening in the middle. It was closed. Eight seconds left. He then reversed himself, spinning back to behind the three-point line. He was gonna try it! It was a rainbow, with the ball's arc soaring high above the top of the backboard. The players, the fans, and 'Nique himself watched open-mouthed as the ball popped through the middle of the net, a perfect swish!

Dominique finished with 49 points, his career high, and we mobbed him on the court. It was quite a Christmas present for the team, and he had gift-wrapped it.

That one basket was an emotional boost that lifted the team more than anyone realized. After the holiday break, we won 10 of our next 14 games, and we even took Boston into overtime. We lost that squeaker, on Larry Bird's 41-point near-perfection performance. But our crowds were picking up, and so was our morale.

Traveling with an NBA team is a real experience, especially when you're winning. Because there are only 13 players on a team (as opposed to, say, 45 on a pro football team), you get close to each other pretty fast. A sample day goes something like this:

You fly into whichever city you happen to be playing in, and you get to fly first class because there are only a few professional basketball players who can fit into a coach-class plane seat. The airlines really pamper you, and sometimes when a beautiful flight attendant is serving me a shrimp cocktail in my first-class seat, I can't help but think back to those days of riding a rickety old bus around the dusty towns of West Texas, when I was back at Midland College.

Anyway, then we take a bus to our hotel and check in. Everyone gets his own room, and if you ever want to figure out which floor the basketball players are staying on, you only have to listen. Five minutes after they've checked in, you'll hear the noise of a dozen jam boxes blaring away, often accompanied by the awful sound of a player who thinks he's singing just as well as Marvin Gaye. Most of the players listen to rap or jazz, and Kevin "Devo" Willis is the team's Grand Rapmaster. Randy Wittman and Scott Hastings, who are inseparable on the road, are usually cranking out some Bob Seger or Bruce Springsteen. Basketball, you see, is a very soulful game, and music is a key element for the professional hoop man.

Usually there's a short practice, about two hours or so, which includes stretching those long muscles, working on free throws (you can never shoot enough of them), doing some outside shooting, and maybe a light scrimmage using some special plays we put in to capitalize on an opponent's weak areas. Then we talk strategy, with Fratello, Reed, and Suhr giving pointers, going over ways to handle certain lineups, and so on. Not to take away anything from the coaches, but by the time you reach the professional ranks, basketball becomes a player's game. Because the game is so lightning fast, it's played by instinct rather than by grand design. Some coaches like to orchestrate every move and control the players, especially if the team is young and undisciplined. My favorite coaches, though, are the ones who "lace 'em up and let 'em play," allowing one group of players to work together for longer periods of play, knowing that when five players are comfortable with each other, they will instinctively lift each other's level of play and put together moves and passes that simply can't be diagrammed. Fortunately, Mike Fratello favors a little of both styles, and of course having an NBA legend like Willis Reed coaching alongside him hasn't hurt. Add Brendan Suhr, a friendly fellow who gets along with the players unusually well, and it seems to me the Hawks have one of the best coaching staffs in the league.

When practice is over, we wander back to the hotel and begin the nightly effort of amusing ourselves. Most guys watch a lot of TV, or read, while others get together in groups and play dice or cards. Sometimes the stakes get pretty high, and I stay away from the poker games. If there's time, we check out the local mall or catch a movie, but basketball players really don't do the sort of late-night carousing at clubs that people might think. For one thing, basketball is just too physically demanding on your body to go out partying all the time. After all, basketball players get paid *lots* of money to perform, and management doesn't let you forget that. If you're slacking off or playing poorly, you can bet that the team's general manager will ask the coaches, "Is Spud getting enough sleep? He looks a little sick out there." Drugs used to be a big problem, and I know there are NBA players who still use them. But the league's antidrug campaign has had a definite impact, and you hear of fewer and fewer guys who have bad drug habits. As for the Hawks, I can't think of one player who has a drug problem: A lot of these guys are so straight I guess you could call them squares. Feel free to count me in.

Being on the road is hardest on the guys who are married. It's just about impossible to bring wives and kids along, because we're never in the same place for more than 48 hours. About half the guys on the team are married, and it's especially tough because being a pro basketball player seems to make it easier for a guy to meet unattached women, if he's interested. That puts a strain on any relationship, and I admire the married guys for keeping things under control.

I look forward to getting married someday, settling down and having kids. I love kids, and I'll probably want three. Kids help keep you young, and their innocence is something the world needs more of. For the time being, though, being single is pretty fun and certainly allows you to concentrate more on your game.

For me, that concentration is key, and at this early stage of my career I was surprised to learn that even the older players had not lost their obsession with discussing basketball. Because there are only 295 professional basketball players in the whole NBA, it's like a very exclusive fraternity and everyone seems to know each other. That's another funny thing about the sport: There's no secrecy to it. In baseball there are elaborate signals flashed from coaches to players and from pitcher to catcher; in football, players huddle up and call plays, while coaches have private phone lines up to the pressbox where tendencies are analyzed and strategies debated. In basketball, though, it's all out in the open. Sure, we've got plays, but every one of our opponents knows exactly what those plays are just as we know theirs. The challenge is, is my team's ability to run the play better than theirs to stop it? Again, it all comes down to raw, naked, physical skill. Great matchups are like the scene in the movie *Billy Jack*, where Billy Jack, a karate expert, looks this thug right in the eye and says, "I'm gonna take this foot, and kick in the head right above your left ear, and there's nothing you can do about it." Before the thug can react, Billy Jack nails him. Well, just imagine Magic Johnson dribbling downcourt and announcing, "Okay, listen up. I'm taking this ball, dribbling right past your lazy ass, and dishing off to Kareem who'll then jam through two points worth of basketball, and there ain't nothing you can do about it." It happens. Confrontation is the essence of the game.

My first 16 weeks of professional ball were everything I dreamed they would be. My teammates, my coaches, the Hawks' staff and fans, all made me feel welcome and I was sitting on top of the world. Wanting more sounds greedy beyond belief, but *still* something greater was lurking out there. In Dallas, on February 8, 1986, my life would change forever. The Saturday of the Slam Dunk contest would be a day to remember.

12

Flying High

I'm standing on the floor of Reunion Arena in Dallas, eyeing the basket for my final dunk and imagining I am 16 years old again. There it is in my memory, that hot summer day seven years ago in a sweathouse gym named Highland Hills, when I summoned all my ability to jump higher and harder than ever before. That was the first time.

The ball is the same, and the basket is still 10 feet tall. But everything else is different. Now there are 17,000 people cheering like crazy and millions more watching on national TV. The game announcers, the judges, and the whole basketball world is not quite convinced; can the little guy do it?

He did, and nobody—least of all Spud Webb—was ready for the onslaught of media attention that was to follow.

Instant fame is an extraordinary thing. Being an athlete, and notable because of my size, I was used to press coverage, but this was nuts! No sooner had the Gatorade people given me the $12,000 check as 1986 Slam Dunk Champion than people ran up to me, screaming like I had just been named president of the United States by appointment. Cameramen were everywhere, and reporters shouted questions and asked for interviews in such a frenzy that I could barely find my family to share the moment. It was wonderful and fun, but it was scary, too.

While I was ushered off to the interviewing room, my agents Bill and Robin Blakeley were already being approached with marketing offers. Robin told me that within five minutes of my winning dunk four different executives and major corporations had come over and asked about using me in promotional campaigns. That whole business world was far away to me at the time, but I would quickly become an expert. As Robin said that night, "Spud, like it or not, you're a national figure now. Everyone is going to want a piece of you, but we'll go through these offers one by one and we won't do anything you're not absolutely comfortable with. So, prepare yourself, because it's about to get real hairy."

One saving grace was that Bill Needle had made the trip from Atlanta to look after me just in case things got crazy. Pretty good thinking on Bill's part, and I owe him a lot because he took over the press requests like the pro he is. After the contest, I finished an interview with Greg Gumbel of ESPN and I was ready to head home with some friends. Bill reminded me of the All-Star Gala that night with Willie Nelson; the p.r. people wanted me to go to the party with Larry Bird and have some pictures taken. Bill was amused because after they took the pictures, I left and went back to my hotel. All that noise and glitter wasn't for me; I wanted to be with my family, and some friends from the neighborhood.

Forgetting the Slam-Dunk hoopla, there was still half a season of basketball yet to play and the Hawks were flying. We had a game down in Houston against the Rockets, and then there was a five-game road trip out to the West Coast again. Bill was a real trooper, setting aside his duties in Atlanta and coming on the trip with us to coordinate all the media requests for what he called the "Spud Over America" tour. For the next 10 days, Bill fielded all my calls (which he said were about 30 a day) and handled all the interview arrangements while I hid out in another room under a different name. My job was easy: Just think basketball.

When I stepped onto the floor of the Summit in Houston, I was a changed man. Where before I had been withdrawn, playing sometimes unsure of myself, now I was totally confident. Even though the Slam Dunk was sideshow material, completely apart from my professional game, the win gave me some unexpected confidence. Suddenly, I was fearless, and back to my old reckless, hard-charging ways. In the first half I was all over the place, trying to put as much pressure on Houston as possible. I scored 13 points in 15 minutes, and just before the halftime buzzer, I nailed my first NBA three-pointer.

After the game, Jeff Denberg strolled over and looked me up and down.

"What's the matter?" I asked.

"I gotta check your height, Spud," he answered. "You shoot three three-pointers in 48 games, missing all three, and suddenly you come out there and nail this one like it was a lay-up. Man, you're playing like you've grown four inches!"

Maybe inside I had. Five nights later in the Salt Palace, I needed every inch I could get. We were playing the Utah Jazz, and it was one of the wildest, most physical games I've ever played in.

Now Utah is no team of wimps, with guys like Mark Eaton and Karl "The Mailman" Malone acting as "the enforcers" inside. Karl was also a Talent Sports International client, and since that company has almost a family atmosphere to it, we became good friends. I think Karl may be the strongest guy in the league, and like most of those Louisiana boys, he doesn't take lip from anybody.

For our part, we were at the end of a nine-game road trip, and when guys are away from their wives and girlfriends that long, they get very surly. From the moment we tipped off, it was a dogfight. Every time I drove the lane, I got hammered, but fortunately I had a good night from the free-throw line, hitting 13 of 14. Everybody was dishing out the blows, and we had Jack Madden as a referee, who a lot of people in Atlanta think is prejudiced against the Hawks. Madden lives just outside Atlanta, and the theory goes that he always calls extra fouls on our team just to show he's not playing favorites. The statistics seem to bear that out: In 1985–86, we lost *seven* straight games Madden refereed, including two play-off games. Finally, the Hawks formally requested he be banned from officiating any more of our games.

But that hadn't happened yet. Yes, Madden was refereeing, and by the fourth quarter, our team looked like the walking wounded. Antoine Carr was at home with a stress fracture in his left leg; Dominique was on the bench with a sprained knee; Tree was out with a bad cut over his eye, and Doc had been ejected by Madden for arguing with a call. As for the fouls, well, Koncak had fouled out, as had Willis, Hastings, and I. Then in overtime, with only five players still eligible on our whole team, Cliff Levingston fouled out. Only four players left!

None of us had ever seen that before, but the NBA rule is that both teams must have five players, so the last player to foul out may return to the game, and his team is assessed a technical foul. Utah hit the foul shot, and went on to win, 109–105. I felt great about my game, hitting for 21 points and grabbing 8 rebounds, my career high on the boards.

Three nights later, we were home in Atlanta and the L.A. Lakers came to town. The game was a sellout, with 16,522 noisy fans crowding the Omni seats. We had won our last two games convincingly, but we had not beaten the Lakers since 1979. With Magic, Kareem, Worthy, and Cooper, they were an awesome machine of fast-breaking basketball talent.

We were ready to run, too, and slowly but surely over the last few games Coach Reed had persuaded me to use my outside shot more. He had noticed that teams were laying off me, waiting for me to drive inside. By taking the jumper, it forced the defender to come out and get closer to me, and the closer the defender was, the easier it was to race past him for a drive. I knew I would get plenty of chances to try Reed's advice since Doc was injured and once again I was starting.

It was a tremendous game, and I have never felt so confident. Sure enough, the Laker guards were giving me room, and I started hitting my jumper. It surprised everyone. The crowd was loving it, and at one point, Dominique stole the ball and zipped it right to me as I went in for a whooping dunk. The local media had been touting us as "Atlanta's Air Force," and I enthusiastically dropped the bomb.

By the fourth quarter, we were controlling the game and Coach Fratello took me out to a rousing ovation. I had scored 23 points, my career high, hitting 9-for-12 with 13 assists, and the Hawks won a huge game, 102–93. We had played our best, and gotten a seven-year monkey off our backs.

The next night we played Cleveland, and I had another big game, with 22 points and 15 assists. I was playing at the top of my form, and for an athlete, there is no greater sense of fulfillment. Not only had I made the NBA, I was excelling in it! That was exciting, yet I found that the better I played, the more I concentrated on winning. Earning respect as a player is one thing, but establishing yourself as a winner is a step beyond. I was learning to focus my mind on that purpose, and no matter who I was playing against, no matter how famous he was or how tight a friend he was, I had to go out and beat him for my team. Even if it was my own brother, I'd try to kill him too. In the rough world of the NBA, you've got to have killer instincts. Get your guy down, then bury him.

I was also learning to be crafty. Smart players will fool you. If they get knocked down, they get up real slow like they're injured or tired, and the minute you relax, they blow right past you. Other players purposely act bored, like they're not into the game. Don't let that look fool you —it's an old trick and it works. The good players are always thinking. . . .

Probably the most exhilarating aspect of my performance was the scoring. I've always wanted to be a big scorer like Doctor J, Michael Jordan, Mark Aguirre, or Bernard King. Those guys who are 6'6" or 6'8"—they *look* like real basketball players. I sometimes dream about being that size and getting in the paint and lighting it up with 30 or 40 points a game. But that's not my role, and you have fit into your team's system. I love to watch other guys score, and I get a kick out of zipping a good pass to Dominique or Randy and seeing them get a bucket. I know I had a part in the scoring, even if it was just making passes. On a team, you've got to find your role and then be comfortable with it. For instance, my buddy Joe Dumars, who plays for Detroit, was the ninth leading scorer in NCAA basketball history, so you know he can shoot the lights out of the basket. But Detroit has two big scoring guns in Adrian Dantley and Isiah Thomas, so Joe has made a place for himself as one of the top defensive guards in the league. I know he wants to score, too, but for now he's playing his role.

My rookie season already had more than its share of highlights, but there was one more to come. Appropriately, it was in my hometown of Dallas, where we were playing the Mavericks. The game was on a Friday night, but I flew into Dallas early Thursday morning for a very special purpose: Wilmer Hutchins High School had declared it "Spud Webb Day."

You can have all that national attention: I'll take the love and affection of my community any day. What those people did for me was amazing, and although I rarely show much emotion in public, I almost cried. The entire school turned out for the ceremony and filled the stands in the gym. All my old teachers like Ramona Jones, unofficial head of the Wilmer Hutchins "Spud Webb Fan Club," came up and hugged me, and the band played as I walked through an honor guard of ROTC students who had crossed sabres over my head. The cheerleaders were cheering, and everyone was raising the roof for their hometown boy.

Dominique and Cliff came with me, and I think it sent them into shock when they saw how the school turned out for me. But that's the kind of community Wilmer Hutchins is—they support their own. In fact, they retired my jersey that day, number 5, and when the principal held it up Cliff started laughing because it looked so small.

"It's like a doll's size, 'Nique!" he screeched. "Do you believe this? They couldn't do more if it was the president!"

I spoke to the crowd, and though I hadn't planned what to say, the words just came flowing out.

"It doesn't seem that long ago that I played in this gym, and even then the thought of an NBA career was just a distant dream. But now that I'm back here, I know that what I learned at this school from these fine teachers helped make that dream come true. I hope all of you will listen to these teachers, and to your parents, and follow the right path. Stay away from drugs, and from those people who'll try to mess you up, because they are losers. You be a winner. And whatever you do, don't lose sight of your dreams, no matter how impossible they may be. Just think about me, and remember: You can be anything you want to be."

I will never forget that day, or the game that followed it that night. Reunion Arena, unquestionably the loudest, rowdiest place in the NBA to play, was packed to its 17,007 capacity, and the Mavericks were fighting for a play-off spot. Our play-off bid was virtually locked up, but Coach Fratello, whose coaching record in Texas was 0–8, pulled me aside in the locker room and said, "Spud, this is your hometown—you know how to handle these cowboys. I know your family and all your friends are here, so show them what you've got."

I intended to. Doc started and played well, but it was Randy Wittman who was stealing the show. Wittman was a Hoosier under Bobby Knight, and he knows how to play tough, gritty basketball in pressure situtations. I couldn't wait to get in, and at the end of the first quarter, Mike gave me the signal. Kevin McCarthy, the Reunion Arena announcer, gave me an enthusiastic introduction and the Dallas crowd went crazy. Just five weeks ago, they had cheered me for my dunking; now I was determined to show that I could play the game of basketball as well.

In the second quarter, I got a steal off Brad Davis and

went coast-to-coast for a big slam dunk. It was bedlam! I mean, so loud that you could stand next to your teammate screaming and he could not hear you. You talk about fun! Forget the measuring tape, when you get crowd support like that you feel 10 feet tall.

The Mavericks were up by one at the half and by the end of the third quarter, the score was dead even. Mike put me in a few minutes into the fourth quarter, with the instructions, "Make something happen, Spud!" I love that advice. It means a coach has faith in your abilities to go out and create something on the floor, and that's exactly what I did. We were under the Mavericks basket when suddenly the ball squirted loose. It was barely bouncing, an easy pickup for me but a long reach for the big guys. Already at three-quarter speed, I scooped up the ball and angled down the right sideline. Pushing the ball ahead of me, I saw the blur of the crowd as I leaned into the drive, beginning to focus on the basket. Feeling that crowd around me, my family and all my buddies from the neighborhood, I took off, soaring like a falcon hard and fierce toward the hoop. As I reached up with the ball, I could not believe how high I was—the rim was in my face! With everything I had, I threw the ball downward, jerking my body back as the ball slammed through.

Anyone turning on their radio would have sworn we were playing in Atlanta. The noise was ear-splitting joy. Over where my family was sitting, Stephanie almost knocked out an entire row of people with the camera swinging around her neck. Next to our bench, a Dallas fan fell out of his chair, pretending to have fainted over the sight. Everywhere, all over that crazy arena, people were celebrating the sport of basketball, and the fact that even a guy their size could play it with gusto.

I finished with 18 points and 10 assists, and Sheriff Fratello earned his Texas spurs with a 107–103 victory. I was happy for him. For me, the school's honor assembly, all the kind words and speeches made for me by my friends, and then the big victory made it one of the most memorable nights of my life.

Public speaking has never been easy for me. I'm a listener more than a talker. I also believe in the old adage: "Better to be silent and be thought a fool, than to open your mouth and remove all doubt." I've seen so many guys get in trouble because of what they said to the media. And once you've said it, it's forever. You can't take it back. That's another reason I always try to keep a clean image, because one little slip and the press blows it up into a big deal. Like it or not, professional athletes are role models, and I think we have a definite responsibility to stay out of trouble with stuff like using drugs, driving drunk, getting into fights, and so on. Kids imitate so much of what we do, and if we can project a positive image to them, then maybe they'll pick up some good habits.

Because of the increased media attention, I realized that I would have to come out of my shell a little. I love joking around with the guys on the team, but I'm not too good at sharing—I try to handle my problems alone. But since everyone wanted to know every little detail about me, I thought about the people who are great speakers and how they communicate. I met Jesse Jackson once, at a PUSH game in honor of Len Bias. Now there's a man who can speak. And Martin Luther King—he must be the greatest speaker who ever lived. I believe God put him here for that purpose, to lead people through his incredible speeches. Words would just flow from him, and he was so intense that he held crowds of thousands mesmerized.

Music is another thing. How do these people come up with these great lyrics? Entertainers amaze me, the way they can stand before huge audiences and sing so perfectly.

I listen to a lot of rap music, and guys like Run–DMC and LL Cool J come up with rhymes and tunes that I could never create in a million years. The surprising thing for me is how these words seem to flow out so effortlessly, when saying how I feel has always been so hard. It's like I said about being shy as a kid; you have all the same feelings as these other people do, but there's just some force that keeps you from spilling it all out. I know that sometimes makes interviewers uneasy, because they're used to asking a question and then hearing the player rattle on for 10 minutes with his answer. As for me, if you didn't ask, I definitely wasn't going to tell you.

But everybody *was* asking. Aside from Johnny Carson, I was on ABC's *World News Tonight* with Stone Phillips, *PM Magazine,* and *Good Morning America.* There were interviews for *Time, Newsweek, Sports Illustrated, Ebony,* and countless newspapers. More promotion offers were pouring in, and the season wasn't even over yet. I signed a deal with Baden basketballs, who created an undersized "Spudball" with my picture on it. Then I signed a deal with Quaker Oats, which put my picture on 35 million boxes of Chewy Granola Bars. Coca-Cola was calling and I did several appearances for them, but as yet no national commercials. I did do some spots for Eveready Energizer batteries, in a promotion to help raise thousands of dollars for new sporting equipment for underprivileged kids. I also became a national spokesperson for the Boys Clubs of America, which meant doing appearances across the country.

There were a few offers I *didn't* take. The Budweiser people called and talked with Robin about a "This Spud's for You" ad campaign, but I nixed that right away. I'm sure Budweiser is a fine company, but I would never promote anything like alcohol or cigarettes; I don't care how much money they offer me. Shortly after that, Bud came out with its big campaign featuring "Spuds MacKenzie." I think it's pretty funny, and it's working real well for them.

Yes, we did hear from the National Potato Growers Association, but I said no to that. I've heard enough potato jokes. There were a zillion jump rope and weight machine companies that wanted me to say that using their product made me a great leaper, but I didn't think that was right. The most interesting offer was from a film group called Pan African Productions, who wanted me to star in a film based on a ghetto kid who has near-magical basketball powers. They said Jim Brown (the ex-NFL star) was the producer, as if that would make it more attractive to me. The movie was full of sex and cussing, and even though they offered me $15,000 I said no way.

All this attention was rewarding, but it was soon over-shadowed by the fact that the Hawks had made the play-offs. We had compiled a 50–32 record, our hottest season since 1979, and the sixth best record in the league that year. More good news was that Dominique won the NBA scoring title, averaging 30.3 points per game.

That title meant a lot to him, and the whole team shared his excitement. Coming out of the University of Georgia as one of the most highly recruited players in college history, Dominique came to the Hawks in 1982 and had to carry the scoring burden from day one. Sportswriters kid him sometimes, paraphrasing Will Rogers by saying, "Dominique never met a shot he didn't like," and it's true that he shoots a lot, but he sure makes some amazing pressure buckets when we need them the most. He's also a heck of a good free-throw shooter, hitting 82 percent from the line.

We would need all of that talent and more in the play-offs. Our first opponents were our archrivals, the Detroit

Pistons. Our teams that year were similar in several ways. Both had young talent with a pair of great veterans anchoring the team. For Detroit, guard Isiah Thomas and forward Adrian Dantley were the real superstars, while my pal Joe Dumars, and others added youthfulness and depth. Most of all, both teams were *very physical*. As one sportswriter put it, "This is not a series to see who will advance; this is a series to see who will survive."

Game 1 is about to start, and as the Omni fills up with fans, Jeff Denberg is on the prowl for a story. He catches Detroit's assistant coach Dick Versace, and asks him, among other things, what he thinks now of that 5'7" kid he cut from rookie camp about nine months ago.

"Okay, I'll be a big man and admit it," said Versace. "We made a mistake with Spud, but remember: Down deep, no matter how encouraging they might have sounded at the time, *nobody* thought Spud could ever make it in the NBA. We cut him for two reasons: First, we had too many guards and second, we didn't think he could shoot from outside."

"Do you think he'll be a factor in the series?" asked Denberg.

"Our two teams are so even," Versace answered. "What scares me is that Spud may steal a game. He's so quick, and he puts real pressure on a defense."

Nothing can prepare you for the intensity of a play-off game. Everything changes. At first, I'd decided to treat this game like any other. But looking around the locker room at the veterans, I saw that they were totally focused, allowing no room psychologically for anything else but this game, and that was new to me.

"It's a whole new season tonight," said Tree. "You better get ready. You're going to see some of these old bodies come alive like you never believed. Everything happens right now. TV cameras everywhere, the crowds going wild on every play, the coaches freaking out—this is where you really learn what pro ball is about."

I had not played all that well against Detroit during the season, and Coach Fratello wasn't sure how I would respond in my first play-off game. Besides, Doc had played great against Detroit, and so I didn't expect to see too much time.

A quick point about Doc Rivers. In any sport, there is always a competition between the starter and the guy behind him, who wants that starting role. Glenn and I have never had a single problem, and it's because he is one of the classiest guys I've ever met. From the very beginning, when I came into camp getting lots of media attention, Glenn was on my side. In talking to the press it was always "Spud this, and Spud that," but Glenn played right along, each time saying something positive, and *he* was the starter! When I played well, he was the first one to congratulate me, and if I played lousy, he'd be there to back me up. How are you going to be jealous of that? What's more, I was beginning to appreciate certain things about my role coming off the bench. When Fratello put me in, it was always to "make something happen," and I love that. And usually, Glenn was able to offer some pointer about how a particular opponent was playing that night, which helped me exploit that weakness when I got in the game.

In my first play-off game, I got 17 minutes, and I made the most of them, scoring 18 points and giving 4 assists. To the delight of everyone in Atlanta, we put away Detroit, 140–122.

Our next game was also in Atlanta, and it may be the best game I ever played against Detroit. Because of my performance in game 1, Mike gave me more time and I used it well. Neither team really took control, and again it was tough and physical, with "mini-fights" breaking out about every five minutes. I knew the Pistons were really into it when I saw Dumars, who rarely shows much emotion on the court, slap a ball away and go in for a vicious dunk. Joe doesn't dunk much, but tonight he was pumped.

So was Dominique. The Human Highlight Film was recording some memories, hitting everything he put up. I was passing off to him like crazy, and three times down the floor our alley-oop worked to perfection. I was driving the lane, too, and getting hammered, but I was also putting Detroit in foul trouble. Once some of Detroit's big men like Bill Laimbeer were on the bench, Dominique led Atlanta's Air Force on a high-flying point binge, scoring a play-off-high 50 points. I had a good night with the stats as well: 19 points, a career-high 18 assists and 7 rebounds. The Hawks took the second game, 137–125.

After the game, I got lots of questions about whether I played harder because Detroit had cut me. I said no, and I meant it. I never played for the Pistons, so I never got to know anyone with the team. If I had played there and been traded, maybe then I would have felt more spiteful. Who knows? But I played my heart out in these games because I had to; everything the veterans had told me about play-off intensity was true, if not an understatement.

It was on to game 3 in Detroit, where we lost. Talk about your home court advantage—the Pistons play in the Silverdome, which is usually set up for *football* games, and they regularly get crowds of 22,000-plus. That's a lot of noise for a basketball game. The sound must be contagious because the Pistons were talking a lot of noise after the game.

"We'll be eating lobster in Boston!" yelled Laimbeer, one of the least-liked Pistons among Hawk players.

"That does it," said Willis, who had battled Laimbeer all night. "Saturday night we kick their ass."

Saturday night, April 25, 1986. The Silverdome is packed, as the Detroit fans sense a comeback. During warm-ups, both teams were eyeing each other like it was a prizefight; the basketball floor was about to become a war zone.

Inside, Kent Benson and Laimbeer squared off against Kevin and Tree. Kelly Tripuka and Earl Cureton fought Dominique, while Dumars and Thomas played tough with Doc and Randy. In all during the series, there were 230 fouls, with seven players thrown out of games. It was no picnic. At the end of regulation, the score was tied. Hello overtime.

The war went on through overtime, and at the end it was *still* tied. We were trying to end it, while the Pistons were fighting for their lives, knowing that this well could be the last game of their season. All the stops were being pulled out, and with just 18 seconds left, the Pistons hit a miracle shot to go up by one. We huddled on the sideline, and planned our next move. I was to keep the ball out high, while a pick was set for Dominique. I would drive the lane, and as I had done all season, dish off to 'Nique at the last second. It was tough to defend against, and Nique was Mr. Cool under pressure.

We inbounded the ball, and I dribbled out above the key as we had planned. The clock ran down . . . 11 . . . 10 . . . 9. . . . As it got to 8, I made my move, juking left then heading back right. Isiah was right there, so I had no place to go but up. I never got there. The Detroit big men were waiting for me, and in their effort to block my path, they fouled me.

It's overtime in my first play-off game and suddenly I'm on the line with my team trailing by one. Everyone in the house knows the season is at stake, and Spud Webb will decide it. Would I be a hero or a goat? My teammates shouted encouragement as the referee handed me the ball. I dribbled twice, took a deep breath, and shot.

I missed.

Wait a minute, that's not what happened the 4,379 times I dreamed about this moment as a kid! In fact, in my childhood fantasy where I'm at the line shooting two, my team behind by one, with the NBA championship on the line, I make both free throws every single time. I'm mobbed by my teammates and carried off on their shoulders. I'm a hero and the whole town loves me.

Now, back to reality. At least I did not crumble when I missed the first bucket. True, there were 20,000 maniacs from Motown screaming at me and hoping my arms would fall out of their sockets, but that shouldn't matter. I just missed the shot.

I still had a chance to tie the game, and send it into a second overtime. I got the ball, and this time I *really* concentrated on my form, trying to correct slightly what had made me miss the first time. I let it fly and . . . bingo! A second overtime.

The next five minutes of play were almost a déjà vu of the first overtime. Hard playing, with the crowd hanging on every shot. With less than 30 seconds left, Dominique hit a spinning jump shot to put us up by one. Detroit's ball. Isiah was working to his right, then he accelerated like a Porsche Turbo and headed toward the baseline, where he angled hard left toward the basket. Scott Hastings was there to stop him, but Isiah spun around in a wild, incredible move and lofted the ball against the backboard with reverse spin. Whoosh. Nine seconds left, and once again we are down by one, 113–112. The ball was back in my hands, and I was heading straight for the hoop when I got fouled again in the lane. It was a two-shot foul, and so here I was once more at the line with the game in my hands.

Detroit called time out to let me think about the shot, and I did. I was thanking God that I had another chance to win this game for my team, and how lucky I was to get a second chance.

I believe in the power of positive thinking. In the first overtime, I was *hoping* to make that first free throw; in the second, I *knew* I was going to make it. I still felt the pressure—all the way to my bones—but I wasn't going to let anything stop me. Stepping up to the line, I didn't look left or right, only straight ahead. As soon as I felt the ball, the tremendous noise of thousands of screaming and stomping fans began to fade away, like someone had turned the volume down in my head. Two bounces. Then another. The shot was away.

And in! My teammates leaped in the air, hands raised. Yes! We had a chance to win, and I wasn't going to blow this one. I felt totally sure it was going in from the minute I fired. Bang! We were up by one!

Detroit inbounded the ball, and passed to Earl Cureton, who shot just as the buzzer sounded. The shot hit high on the glass and bounced away. We were going to Boston!

In the madness that followed, my boyhood dream came true. I was mobbed by my teammates, and they hugged me so hard I almost lost my breath. What a feeling that is! Everything you've worked for together all season long, all the blood, sweat, and emotion is in that hug of joy. You love your teammates at that moment with all your heart, because they too gave everything they had to win. In the locker room, our haven from the world, the hugs and hollering continued. You only get about 10 minutes alone as a team before the press comes pouring in, and suddenly it's public again. You savor those few minutes, and looking into the eyes of my teammates I felt proud to be with them.

I have to admit I was proud of myself, too. I made it

into the NBA on the slimmest of chances, but I made it. And while I made more than my share of mistakes, I proved once and for all that I could play. Then finally, to sink the winning baskets in my first NBA play-off series, well, it was greater than anything I could ever have dreamed. I knew then that all my efforts, as a kid in South Dallas until this day, were worth it. Every workout, every game, even every on-court embarrassment was worth it. Sacrifice makes success sweet.

We left the Silverdome a closer, stronger team. And for a moment, we forgot that we were pro basketball players, and just acted like a bunch of college guys. Winning is satisfying, but it is also loads of fun, and we made the most of it.

13

The Long and the Short of It

At long last, Stan Kasten was a believer. After all those weeks when he refused to take me seriously (Kasten dreamed up "Spud Webb Stamp Night," claiming I was too small to fill up a poster; he also petitioned the league to change my number to ".4" instead of 4, saying that a guy my size didn't need a whole number), Stan came around full circle and is now one of my biggest fans.

One indication of that came in Boston, where we were set to play the Celtics for the Eastern Conference semifinals. Stan was wearing a button that read "That Spud Webb—He Can Play," and saying that our quick, strong team was ready to put away the Celtics. The players felt the same way; we thought we matched up well against Boston, and we went into the Boston Garden with no fear.

A lesson in respect came quickly. Boston showed why they had a phenomenal 67–15 regular season record, whipping us twice in Boston and then a third time in Atlanta. Down 3–0, we faced the humiliation of being swept 4–0 in front of our home crowd.

What's more, game 4 was to be played Sunday afternoon in front of a national TV audience. Former Celtic coach Tom Heinsohn was doing the "color" work on the broadcast, and I don't think he had seen me play much, because he seemed pretty amazed at my play the entire afternoon. I was playing with total abandon, drawing on the energy from the Omni crowd and giving every last ounce, knowing that this was very possibly the last game of my rookie season. I wanted something to remember.

After driving inside a few times, I noticed Dennis Johnson was playing pretty far off me, respecting my speed. Remembering what Coach Reed had told me, I started pulling up and taking the jumper. And they were going in. I had one big steal that might have led to a dunk, but as I dribbled past Danny Ainge, he grabbed me by the shorts and tugged. You can't go too far when a guy's pulling on your shorts. Seeing the tape, it looks pretty funny, but I had a lot of people ask me, "Why didn't you punch Danny Ainge when he grabbed you? *Somebody* ought to deck him!"

I disagree. How can you criticize the way he plays? He hits open shots, passes off to his teammates, and dives for loose balls. I admire that. Everybody in the NBA fights from time to time, and just because Ainge isn't going to take any junk off anybody is no reason to get on him.

Nothing Ainge or Bird or McHale could do was going to stop the Atlanta Air Force that day. After nine consecutive defeats from Boston going back to 1983, we finally buried the jinx with a 106–94 victory. I ended my dream season with a very satisfying total of 21 points, 12 assists and 6 rebounds in 24 minutes of play. The Celtics went on to win the world championship, and I went back to Dallas to be with my family.

Postseason honors poured in for our team. Coach Fratello was named Coach of the Year, Stan Kasten won Executive of the Year, and Dominique was named to the All-Star team. I made second-team All-Rookie to go along with my slam-dunk title. One of the most gratifying things for me, though, was playing two of my best games against the Lakers and the Celtics. Playing with and beating the very best—that's what it's all about.

With the successful season came more marketing offers. I renewed my contract with Pony for two years at $250,000 and signed a deal with Church's Fried Chicken to promote their "Spud Webb Meal Deal," which is a chicken wing, small fries (don't laugh, now), and a small Coke. I also did a poster for Sunkist, where I'm slam dunking an orange and I did radio spots for a very tasty snack food called "Break Cakes." For that one, I worked with a voice coach to help get rid of my Texas accent.

The summer brought more satisfying moments. I appeared on the *Donahue* show in New York with outstanding people like W. Clement Stone and Richard Anderson of *Parade* Magazine. The theme was "Achievers—People Who Overcame Obstacles," and the discussion was fascinating. I love hearing how other people who were underdogs worked their way to the top.

Before the show, one of the *Donahue* staffers asked me about prejudice. He wondered if my pro-basketball-star status made me immune to racial problems.

I said no. There is prejudice everywhere, and though some people talk about it like it was in the past they're dead wrong—it's still around. That's frustrating because so many people both black and white have worked to change those attitudes. Still, I don't sit around worrying about it, I just leave it alone and ignore those who aren't smart enough to realize that skin color tells nothing about the person inside.

As athletes, I think we do a lot to show America that you don't need hatred. White and black, we play together, work together. When any one of us does well, the other guys congratulate him as an equal; when one player falls, the others are there to help him up. I hope when young kids see this they understand that races can get along if they leave that "I'm better than you" garbage with their grandparents. Success is out there for *all* of us, and the more society works as one big "team" of different people instead of clashing as minority versus majority, the more we can accomplish.

Over the summer I did more than 50 appearances around the country. I met all types of people and had some incredible experiences. At one appearance for Baden basketballs in Iowa City, Iowa, more than 8,000 kids showed up. Can you believe that? I love rapping with kids, because they're still innocent and hopeful about the world. They get excited about little things the way I do, and they tell me about their dreams, the same kind of dreams I had growing up.

Kids represent simple pleasures to me. Give a kid an autograph, or a basketball tip, and he's on cloud nine for the rest of the week. That's why I put on basketball camps over the summer, working with hundreds of kids all over Dallas, because the kids make you feel so appreciated! I just can't do enough for them, because I know a lot of kids don't have the benefit of a great home life like I did. I believe that "to whom much is given, much is expected," and I have a responsibility to share my time and talents with kids, the same way my sister Renee does as an elementary school teacher. One fun way I do that is through my annual "Spud Webb All-Star Game" held in Dallas which benefits the Boys Clubs.

It's an idea Robin Blakeley and the TSI crew came up with, and so far we've raised over $75,000 for the Dallas area Boys Clubs. Players like Magic Johnson, Rolando Blackman, Ron Harper, and Waymon Tisdale have played along with numerous others in a benefit game such as the one Magic puts on every year to raise money for the United Negro College Fund. It's slammin', jammin' high-octane street ball with very little defense, and it gives players from other teams a chance to relax and have fun together. I think pro sports needs more of that, and the fans love it.

One thing that never ceases to amaze me is the things people will do for pro athletes. Fans can be an intrusion sometimes, but they also send things to you like you were related or something. Young girls write me asking advice about their boyfriends. Kids of all ages draw elaborate portraits of me and send them, along with stuffed animals, T-shirts, food, flowers, hats, you name it. People have composed songs for me, like "Go Spud Go," "Little Man," "The Dunkmaster," and "Jammin' Just Like Spud." The last two were so good that the Hawks played them over the Omni p.a. system during warm-ups before games.

And the mail. There's so much of it, it's hard to read it all but I try. During the season, I get about 200 letters a week, sometimes more. That's over 6,000 a year, not counting the summer. I swore if I ever got famous I would always answer my mail, but I never considered anything like this—you can only do so much, but you appreciate every single letter.

One letter I received from the City of Atlanta was very special. It was an invitation to be Grand Marshal of the Fourth of July Parade through downtown Atlanta. What's more, I would have a pretty impressive man beside me as co–Grand Marshal: Vice President George Bush. Now, I was supposed to go eat barbecue that day with Mookie and some friends, but what the heck, I love a parade.

At the last minute, Vice President Bush was called away on some important business. But I did get to meet Atlanta mayor Andrew Young, who I really admire. He has done great things for the city, and I hope I play my whole career here because Atlanta is my favorite of all the cities I've visited. The people are friendly, the climate is great, and if this sounds like a plug for the city, well, it is.

One other major thing happened to me that summer: I became a millionaire. After a month of negotiating, I signed a four-year deal with the Hawks good for more than $1 million in salary and incentives. And for the very first time in my entire career, I knew I didn't have to prove myself to make the team.

The first thing I did was to retire my mom. She had worked her heart out taking care of six kids and now it was our turn. That may have been the greatest moment of my basketball career.

The next season brought even more success for the Hawks, as we finished with a fantastic record of 57–25 and won the Central Division. It was a team that rewrote the record books in many ways, with Dominique, Kevin, Doc, and Randy all having tremendous seasons. Unfortunately for me, I saw most of it from the sidelines.

After overcoming just about every obstacle imaginable in my basketball career, God brought me another test: a major injury. After starting the season hot as a pistol, I strained my knee on a freak play against the Indiana Pacers. I tried to get up, but it hurt like hell and began swelling like somebody was pumping it full of air. Our trainer, Joe O'Toole, is one of the nicest, most positive guys around, but I could tell by the look on his face when he saw my knee that I was in trouble.

The next day the Hawks sent me to see some specialists, and the news was not good: I had a torn lateral meniscus, and it required surgery. Surgery! Every pro athlete dreads going under the knife, but I felt better when the doctors told me it would be arthroscopic surgery, which was not nearly as serious or difficult as some other knee operations. The surgery was set for two weeks away.

My knee ached, but it wasn't the pain that bothered me —it was the uncertainty. How long would I be out? The Hawks were now 18–4. What if they went on to win the championship without me? What if I lost my leaping ability? A thousand questions raced through my mind. At least I'm still young, I told myself, and I know my body can bounce back if things aren't too broken up.

Two days before Christmas, 1986. I went into surgery at Hughston Sports Medicine Clinic in Columbus, Georgia. When I awoke late that afternoon, the doctor brightened up my holiday by telling me the operation went well, and with a solid rehab program I might see some action toward the end of the season.

I used to think that playing badly gives you the worst feeling as an athlete, but after "riding the wood" for over half a season, I know that poor play takes a distant second. Being injured, unable to contribute and be a part of the action, is the toughest thing to bear. Game after game I would sit at the end of the bench in my street clothes, feeling totally depressed. Sure, you cheer for your teammates who are out there battling, but you also feel useless. I hated that feeling, and I worked my butt off rehabilitating my knee so I could get back in uniform.

My first game back was against the Dallas Mavericks at Reunion Arena in Dallas. All of my family was there with lots of my friends, and I felt an extra surge of excitement when Coach Fratello signaled me to go in and a huge roar went up from the Dallas crowd. I was playing again! It felt like I had been released from prison, and I was all over the court. We beat the Mavericks, not an easy feat in Reunion Arena, for our ninth win in a row. We were streaking for the play-offs.

We started things off by stomping the Indiana Pacers, three games to one. Then we headed to Detroit to face our archrivals the Pistons, where we promptly became the stompees. The Pistons took our best-of-seven series 4–1, and we were left wondering what happened.

With 20–20 hindsight I think our problem was still inexperience. We were young and hungry, but we were looking around, waiting to see what the other team would throw at us. In the NBA, you have to go out there and *take it*. You can't wait for the other guy to throw the first punch. We did against Detroit, and we got KO'ed.

NBA veteran. I like the sound of that. And if you'll excuse the pun, I think I did a lot of growing up in my third year. It started out slow, because Doc Rivers was having an unbelievable year, and I didn't get many minutes. It was worth it to see Doc named to the All-Star squad, though, because he really deserved the recognition. I was there in Chicago for the All-Star Weekend, which might have been renamed the "Michael Jordan Basketball Exhibition" since he was the big story.

I took a case of the flu and a bum knee into the Slam Dunk Contest, which I didn't feel like doing, but there was so much media hype about the '85, '86 and '87 winners being there (Dominique, myself, and Jordan) that I said okay. I was eliminated early, and the finals came down to Jordan and 'Nique. Who won? Dominique won it by a mile. Who got the trophy? Michael Jordan, because the hometown judges were not about to give it to anybody else. 'Nique walked off the floor shaking his head, saying, "Well, this is Michael's town and his show. What are you gonna do?" Jordan is so exciting, and it was hard to get too angry because you naturally pull for a guy like that. He also won the All-Star MVP award, which made the show complete. But next year, the Dunk Contest is in Houston, and it will be a different story. Next year I'm gonna win it.

The Slam Dunk Contest is where all the crazy media attention began for me, and I couldn't help but think about that when we ran into the Washington Bullets this year during preseason in Baltimore. It was the first time I was going to play against a guy shorter than I am.

Being the new "Smallest Man in the NBA," Mugsy Bogues was getting the tidal wave of media attention that I had gotten two years earlier. I knew Mugsy from my NC State days, and I took a minute before the game to give him some advice on handling the media. In every city, the media people are different; some are pros who are looking for facts, and others are hackers, looking for gossip and dirt. Unfortunately, *all* of them ask the same stupid question: "How does it feel to be the smallest player in the NBA?" That one was Mugsy's to answer now, and I was more than happy to let somebody else have the honor. And since Mugsy is only 5'3", it feels good to look *down* on someone for a change!

Do Bogues and Webb represent a trend toward smaller players in the NBA? I don't think so. It remains to be seen how successful Bogues might be, but the fact that little guys like Michael Adams of Denver (5'10") and myself have been able to contribute does mean that there is still a place in pro ball for small players, if they are quick and play smart.

You also have to be tough, because the NBA gets more brutal every year. The players not only get bigger every year, they get meaner, with musclemen like Karl Malone and Charles Barkley becoming stars. Those guys weigh 260. I weigh 130. Makes you think, doesn't it? I think eventually they will have to widen the court, which will help us fast guys, but I hope they don't raise the basket as long as I'm playing. I don't think I can get my vertical leap up to five feet.

It's playoff time, and I'm sitting here watching the Pistons and the Lakers go at it for the 1988 NBA World Championship. These are two great teams, but I can't help thinking that the Hawks should be there. We had a great season, and a good playoff series, beating Milwaukee convincingly and then heading up to Boston Garden to meet the Celtics. Even though we were without backup center Jon Koncak and my buddy John Battle was hurt, we gave a gutsy effort in Boston. Coming back to Atlanta, a sellout crowd was in place along with a national TV audience to see if our team could pull off an upset.

We played our hearts out, and I had a great game. Against Milwaukee, I had jumped off two legs for the first time since my injury, and I felt the old leaping ability come back 100 percent. So against the Celtics, I was running the floor and driving to the hole like the Spud of old—it felt like flying! With the game getting tight at the end of the third quarter, we called time-out with just 10 seconds to go. We set up a play and when the ball came to me, I pulled up behind the 3-point line . . . and nailed it! The Omni crowd went wild, and it was something fun for my friends watching on CBS.

In the fourth quarter, Boston started coming back, but I hit three straight jump shots to keep us safely ahead. When you're dropping shots like that you feel on top of the world—bulletproof! Most importantly, we won the game, and for my 11 points and 13 assists I was named Player of the Game by the CBS announcers. But even that wasn't enough for us. We came back the next night and whipped

Larry Bird & Company again. This time I had 17 points and 3 assists in 20 minutes, and our whole bench, including Cliff Levingston and Antoine Carr, played great. Leading the way was the "old man" himself, Tree Rollins, who led the whole team with hustle and guts against the Celtic centers.

We then beat Boston in Boston and had a chance to take the series, leading 3–2 with Game 6 at the Omni. Losing that one (and eventually, the series) was heartbreaking. Sitting in the locker room, everybody was thinking to themselves, "If I'd just done one extra thing we might have won it." Those thoughts stay on your mind for a long time.

When the season ended, it was announced that our assistant coach Don Cheney was headed to Houston. I was happy for him, but sad to see him go, just as I was sad to see Willis Reed leave. Both are great men and smart coaches; I think the quality of play in the league is much better today because so many great players have stayed on to become great coaches themselves. I think I might enjoy that myself one day.

Whatever happens, I'd love to stay in basketball. Even now, with three years of pro experience under my belt, I still get those tingles, those same feelings you get as a little kid, when I walk out onto the court before an NBA game. I look around at the players, studying who is on the floor, and I drink up the atmosphere of the moment: the thousands of fans, the nervous coaches, the cameras and referees, and the whole spectacle. I think about how far I've come to get here, and I remind myself not to ever take anything for granted. I've got to work harder every year, getting even more pumped up to play the game I love.

I still have big goals, and being little won't stop me. It never has, because I believe you can accomplish *anything* you set your mind to, even if the world says you can't. There are exciting things ahead for me, I know that, and I thank God for setting that path for me. For now, that path is playing the world's greatest game with the world's greatest players, and getting paid for it. Remarkable!